BARELY HANGING ON

A CAREGIVER'S PLIGHT

LEE HILDEBRANDT

BALBOA
PRESS
A DIVISION OF HAY HOUSE

Balboa Press books may be ordered through booksellers or by contacting:

Balboa Press
A Division of Hay House
1663 Liberty Drive
Bloomington, IN 47403
www.balboapress.com
1 (877) 407-4847

Because of the dynamic nature of the Internet, any web addresses or links contained in this book may have changed since publication and may no longer be valid. The views expressed in this work are solely those of the author and do not necessarily reflect the views of the publisher, and the publisher hereby disclaims any responsibility for them.

The author of this book does not dispense medical advice or prescribe the use of any technique as a form of treatment for physical, emotional, or medical problems without the advice of a physician, either directly or indirectly. The intent of the author is only to offer information of a general nature to help you in your quest for emotional and spiritual well-being. In the event you use any of the information in this book for yourself, which is your constitutional right, the author and the publisher assume no responsibility for your actions.

Any people depicted in stock imagery provided by Thinkstock are models, and such images are being used for illustrative purposes only. Certain stock imagery © Thinkstock.

Print information available on the last page.

ISBN: 978-1-5043-6050-0 (sc)
ISBN: 978-1-5043-6049-4 (hc)
ISBN: 978-1-5043-6053-1 (e)

Library of Congress Control Number: 2016909986

Balboa Press rev. date: 08/09/2016

Robert and Lee (1996)
15th Anniversary Photo

This book is dedicated to
all caregivers everywhere

and to the memory of
Robert, with love

AN INVITATION

I INVITE YOU TO TAKE a journey with me. This invitation includes multiple types of people: those who are in and approaching their retirement years, those who have parents in their retirement years who are in good health, and those who have parents with impaired health.

I wish I could describe my husband's and my journey in the glowing adjectives of a tour brochure, with words such as *fabulous, breathtaking,* and *invigorating,* but those words just don't apply. However, I do hope you'll find our venture meaningful, informative, helpful, and worthwhile to you.

I want you to travel with me back in time as I relate my experiences of the last four years. During that time, my spouse, Robert, went from a completely independent lifestyle to one of total dependence and incapacity, both physically and mentally.

We traveled into the maze of Adult Protective Services, Medicaid and its spend-down requirements, nursing home living, estate planning, home health assistance, legal issues of guardianship, hospice care, and various other related topics. I made the original journey mostly alone, in the dark, and functioning primarily in crisis mode for the entire trip.

As I tried to navigate the maze of health care agencies, I had to seek out resources and assistance as best I could. There were no guidebooks to help me or to point me in the right direction. Friends would offer information, but it was often incorrect. This made things even more difficult for me. I was flying blind for the most part, and that made me feel anxious, frustrated, and very vulnerable. It was a stressful ordeal to live through.

I'm a registered nurse and a clinical specialist in adult psychiatric and mental health. I'd been working in the health care for more than twenty years. Wouldn't you think that would prepare me to take care of my husband? I found my training and background helpful in many ways, but I felt stretched to my very limit most of the time—and sometimes even beyond. I wondered how people survive in these circumstances when they have *no* background or experience to draw from.

My purpose in writing about my experiences is to help you have a smoother, less stressful journey should you find yourself in some or all of the situations described. My hope is to provide a ready source of information that will give support and guidance should you have to make such a journey.

I've tried to provide a general overview of some of the agencies you may want to contact for assistance and/or information and some that you may be forced to engage with by necessity rather than by choice. This information is general rather than specific, because each state has its own health care guidelines, standards, and rules. However, I'm hopeful that if you can follow the broad path, it will provide the support you need to proceed on your journey and make the tough decisions required with some confidence and an element of control.

Bon voyage!

THE DIAGNOSIS

. . . .

It was February of 2004, and my husband, Robert, and I were in the doctor's office, talking with our new primary care physician. Our previous doctor, Dr. Achebe, had moved to another state to teach at a medical school. Robert had liked her very much. Our new doctor had been in town for a while, and she came highly recommended. Robert also preferred female doctors. He said they listened to him more, treated him like a person, and didn't talk down to him, which he felt most male doctors did.

We hadn't seen a doctor for some time after Dr. Achebe left; it may have been nearly a year. We had made this appointment to find out why Robert was having problems with his balance. He just wasn't steady on his feet anymore; he often felt as if he were going to fall. Also, he had bouts of uncontrollable shaking in his right hand and arm. The tremors weren't constant, but they seemed to be increasing in frequency.

Dr. Spruce interviewed both of us, assessed Robert, and then gave us her opinion. "I suspect you have Parkinson's disorder. You're showing the classic signs and symptoms. I want you to see a neurologist to confirm the diagnosis, and he'll develop an appropriate treatment plan for you. He will probably start you on some medications to help control the symptoms. Also, I think you might find it helpful to go to the tai chi classes held at the senior center. The exercises may help you to strengthen your muscles and delay the progress of some of the Parkinson's symptoms."

We left the doctor's office and went to McDonald's for a cup of coffee. We were there in time for Robert to interact with the Geezer Group, as they called themselves—ten to fifteen retired elderly who had come from very diverse backgrounds. Their camaraderie was reminiscent of their time spent in military barracks, in locker rooms, or in coffee breaks at work. They met each day to swap war stories from their military experience, share jokes and Internet words of wisdom, solve the world's problems, and keep each other abreast of changes in their health and that of their wives or housemates.

As Robert visited with his friends, I wondered how we would feel had we not been prepared to hear the doctor's diagnosis. Would we have been in a state of shock? Would we have felt angry or very depressed? Parkinson's disease doesn't have a hopeful prognosis. It's a chronic and progressive neurological illness that can mean loss of control of bodily functions, immobility, loss of speech, difficulty swallowing, and much more. There is no cure; the best hope is to gain some element of control and minimize or slow the progression of debilitating symptoms.

As a nurse, I knew this, but as his wife, I was hopeful that the worst scenario wouldn't happen and the disease would progress very slowly. Anyway, that's what I told myself (surely with a strong element of denial).

I also tried to prepare Robert for hearing his diagnosis so he wasn't surprised by it. We had talked about his symptoms many times as they became more obvious, and I had suggested that he might be developing Parkinson's. In my psychiatric practice, many of my patients had been male veterans with various neurological diagnoses. I had noticed the accumulation of Robert's signs and symptoms and had checked the Internet for additional information. I had shared some of this information (only some) with Robert.

As I watched him drinking his coffee, I wasn't sure how much denial he was dealing with, but outwardly, he seemed to have an attitude that matched his favorite motto: "Do the best with what you have to work with, and *be satisfied.*"

I had also mentioned my observations to our children to prepare them for the possibility of a Parkinson's diagnosis. I explained to them the debilitating nature of the disorder. It had been five years since we had moved to the Southwest from Florida, and five of our six children were still living there, while one son was living on the West Coast. They didn't see us frequently, and I felt the changes that were occurring might be a little overwhelming without any prior knowledge. Also, I wanted them to realize that since Parkinson's is progressively debilitating, it would decrease their options for interacting with their dad. Therefore, they might feel that plans for visiting sooner rather than later would be appropriate.

I'd had quit my part-time job in January, a month before the diagnosis, so I could be more available to Robert. I had been working three days a week at our local behavioral health clinic as an intake admissions specialist. I liked the work and my colleagues very much, but I wanted to have as much quality time as I could get with my best friend, soul mate, and husband before Parkinson's took him away from me.

FYI Commentary

When you observe in a loved one or yourself subtle mental or physical changes or an inability to function in the usual manner, and these changes persist for more than two to three weeks or suddenly get worse, you need to check with a primary care physician. If you or your loved one is experiencing sudden pain or the changes are dramatic, you should see a doctor even sooner.

If your doctor gives a diagnosis of a life-threatening or terminal condition, it's prudent to get a second opinion, especially if the disorder can't be confirmed by a diagnostic test, as in the case of Parkinson's disorder. Some diagnoses are based on an accumulation of observed behavior changes and are a best guess by the doctor.

If the second opinion concurs with the first, the probability increases that both doctors are correct. However, if the two doctors don't agree, you should seek a third opinion to get at least a consensus. The same is true for risky procedures and treatments: get more than one opinion about the best way to proceed. Doctors can make mistakes, and you must be proactive where your loved one's health and possibly his or her life are concerned.

BEING PREPARED

. . . .

ROBERT AND I HAD TRIED to be prepared for the realities of aging. We actually started our plans for retirement in the 1990s while living in Florida. He was retired and had just turned sixty. I was fifty-five and still working. We consulted a financial planner, who guided us in making a long-range plan for economic security in our golden years. Robert had retired from a federal government job many years earlier on a Civil Service disability pension. I was working for the Veterans Administration (VA) health care system.

Robert's pension was about one-third of my salary at the time. My salary was above the national average, and I was saving 10 percent off the top in a government retirement plan. We tried to live mostly on my salary and save the majority of his pension income.

Each time we accumulated some funds, we would pay off credit debt. Our debts weren't excessive but were dampening our ability to save because of their high interest rates. Once we had our credit debts paid, we started saving to pay off our house mortgage. Our plan was to enter our golden years debt-free so we could live on our retirement money with less worry about big monthly payments on housing or cars. About a year or so before I retired at age sixty-two, we were debt-free.

Another aspect of our plan was to accumulate savings to provide funds to supplement my income in the event Robert passed away. He had been single when he retired on disability, so he hadn't opted for deductions from his retirement pension to provide for a widow's survivor payment. My pension and Social Security monies combined would be only about 40 percent of Robert's Civil Service pension, and we felt I would have trouble making ends meet on such a small income. So I was working, and we were saving as much as possible for my retirement years in case I were to be widowed. Our accumulated savings would provide the buffer and security I would need if I outlived Robert.

We both had good federal health care insurance plans. However, Robert didn't have Medicare coverage. His government job excluded him from participation because of a possible conflict of interest. Once I became eligible for Medicare, I was able to enroll him in Part A only as my spouse. Since he was a veteran, Veterans Administration health care services were also available to him on a limited basis. We felt these multiple coverages would adequately provide for our health care needs as we grew older.

We prepared wills for the distribution of our assets in the event of our deaths and living wills for our health care needs in the event of our incapacity. We gave each other power of attorney for both financial and health matters and stated the beneficiaries of our estate.

We felt good about our plans. We thought they would provide the security necessary to make our later senior years at least comfortable financially. We felt our health care needs would be met when the changes that come with aging arose. We felt prepared for our golden years.

After I retired, we moved to New Mexico. We found that each state had its own rules and regulations regarding wills and health care documents. So we went to see a lawyer again. This time we had a revocable living trust drawn up and new documents for health care power of attorney formulated. Both Robert and I had been married previously, and each of us had three children. We had no children together. We had been married nearly twenty years by the time we moved to New Mexico. We wanted to provide for all six children equally if we were both killed in an automobile accident or some similar event.

FYI Commentary

So, just what is a revocable living trust?

A revocable living trust is a flexible and adaptable legal document for the management of assets. The person who establishes the trust is called the grantor or original trustee. In our case, since we established the trust as a couple, we were co-trustees. The trust itself is a fictitious legal entity (with a name that you choose) into which you put your assets: real estate, vehicles, saving and checking accounts, money management and mutual fund accounts, etc. Your assets are simply retitled to the trust and therefore to you as the trustee. You retain control over all your property and other assets during your lifetime, and you decide how they will be distributed upon your death. This trust can be amended, added to, changed, or revoked by the person or persons who establish it.

One advantage of a living trust is that it doesn't have to go through probate proceedings, as does a will. Probate procedures make the information of your will public, and your assets actually belong to the court temporarily. The court must determine the validity of the document, supervise the payment of all debts and taxes, and oversee the distribution of your estate to the named beneficiaries. This can be a long process that's expensive and emotionally traumatic to family members.

A living trust is private and immediate, and it ensures your loved ones receive the whole estate without incurring lawyer and court fees. It also may reduce or eliminate estate taxes. Another important aspect of a living trust is that you're appointing someone else (a person of your choice) to handle your trust should you become incapacitated (for example, from a stroke, Alzheimer's, or an accident). No court actions are required.

There are many additional benefits of a revocable living trust, but this gives you some idea of its purpose and advantages. Specifics of a living trust vary from state to state, so you will need to check on what your state of residence requires.

Regardless of which vehicle you choose for the management of your assets upon your death or upon becoming incapacitated, it's vital to the protection of your estate that you make written, legal provision for its distribution. When's the best time to do that? Now!

What is a living will, or health care power of attorney?

Another important document to have completed while you're of sound mind and in relatively good health is a living will, or health care power of attorney. A living will states your preferences should you be in a terminal condition or in an irreversible coma. You may opt for all life-saving procedures to be administered, for no cardiopulmonary resuscitation (CPR), no feeding tube, no antibiotics, no IVs, or various combinations of those.

You also designate someone as your health care power of attorney to make decisions should you be in a coma or become incapacitated in another way. This document, often called an advance directive, is similar to the one that you complete prior to surgery or certain procedures (such as a colonoscopy or endoscopy). However, that advance directive may be specific to that procedure or surgery. It usually stays with your chart at the facility where the procedure or surgery occurred and may not apply to or be available for other circumstances where similar decisions are necessary.

Your primary care physician should have a copy of your living will, as should the person who is your health care power of attorney. This document can be changed or revoked at any time. A living will document may vary somewhat from state to state, so it should be kept current with your present state of residence.

A living will provides for the implementation of your desires regarding your mental and physical health, just as a living trust enables you to express your wishes for the distribution of your material assets. Both documents allow you to designate a person of your choice to act in your stead should you not be able to do so because you've become incapacitated. One never knows when such an event might occur. So again, the best time to prepare your will, your living trust, and your living will for health care is *now*, when you don't yet need it.

ADAPTING TO THE DIAGNOSIS
· ·

THE NEXT YEAR SEEMED TO go by quickly. We were kept very busy with activities related to Robert's diagnosis. We had monthly appointments with the neurologist, who started Robert on the gold-standard medication for Parkinson's: Sinemet. It seemed to help control his symptoms for a while; but before long, the effectiveness wore off. So the doctor ordered an additional medication. When that combination was no longer effective, he tried an entirely different drug. Some worked better than others, and some kept working for a longer period than others. But many of the medications had harsh side effects, so it became a trade off. Did the benefits outweigh the negative side effects? We remained ever hopeful. Robert was compliant with the doctor's recommendations, and we were positive that a workable combination would be found.

There were also appointments with Dr. Spruce, our primary care physician. Robert had been diagnosed with diabetes in 1990 and had been very successful in managing it. He exercised and lost weight, and when we moved to New Mexico, he no longer needed to take medications to control his blood sugar. However, as the Parkinson's progressed, he wasn't able to be as physically active and had to start taking medications again to maintain adequate control.

He was also taking medications for bipolar disorder and had been stable on those meds for fifteen years. They worked well for him and allowed him to function normally and remain symptom-free. He was very compliant with his medication regimen for both the diabetes and the bipolar disorder. He faithfully took his finger sticks and his medications without complaint. But the number of medication bottles on his bathroom shelf seemed to be growing exponentially. We joked that we would be wealthy if we owned stock in pharmaceutical companies.

Dr. Spruce referred Robert to a physical therapist, with whom he had appointments once a week for about twelve weeks. He learned exercises that would help him retain his muscle strength and improve his coordination and balance. He would learn the exercise at the appointment (for example, tossing a ball to each other or standing and walking with good body alignment), and we would do them together at home.

Robert had tai chi classes twice a week, and I went with him to support his effort. I also felt tai chi would help relieve my stress and improve my muscle strength and coordination. Robert had quite a bit of trouble with the exercises because of his impaired balance, so he worked with a chair for assistance and safety. Finally, he didn't want to go anymore. I think he was afraid of falling, although he wouldn't admit that.

We joined a local Parkinson's support group, which met once a month for an hour. The attendance averaged about twelve people. A representative from the National Parkinson's Association officially led the group, though it was a two-hour drive for her each way. She shared information regarding different medications and treatments that were proving effective, resources we might find useful, informational seminars on Parkinson's, and other related information.

It was quite a diverse group. Some of the members had had Parkinson's for many years, and some, like my husband, were newly diagnosed. The ages ranged from a woman in her forties to another in her late eighties. The couples usually consisted of a diagnosed male with his spouse.

We sat around a big oval conference table in a room at the New Mexico State Veterans Home and shared our feelings, frustrations, and experiences over the past month. It was very therapeutic for us, helping us to see our situation in a bigger context so we didn't feel so isolated living with the diagnosis. It helped to get tips and suggestions that others had discovered were useful for them. Sometimes the group went out to lunch after the meeting at a nearby restaurant.

We also made an addition to our family that year. About three years earlier, Robert had wanted to get a dog, but I had vetoed the idea. I knew I would be the caregiver for any pet. And since I was working, I didn't have the time to care for a dog. So we got a kitten. We named her Precious, and she was. She and Robert became great buddies. She would nuzzle in his beard and then fall asleep on his chest. She also accompanied him to the yard as he tended his garden.

She became quite a hunter and would often be out all night hunting. One night, however, she didn't come back. The vet told us that she was probably prey for an owl or hawk. Both of us felt her loss deeply. We decided never to have another cat while living in that area of New Mexico.

Well, soon I was no longer working. So, after Robert was diagnosed, I agreed to get a dog. He wanted a black Lab, because he'd had a black Lab before I met him and had loved her very much. I had never been a dog owner and really didn't know a thing about the care for and feeding of a dog—especially a big dog like a Lab. Truth be known, I was a little afraid of dogs, particularly big ones. But I felt a dog would be a good companion for Robert and a comfort to him when his activity level and mobility declined.

We decided we wanted a female, an older dog that was already housebroken and, hopefully, trained. We thought we might be able to find one at the local pound, and we told our friends what we were thinking about, in case one of them knew of such a dog. I also decided to ask my Higher Power to find us "an appropriate dog." I felt since I was such a novice, I would leave it in the hands of the universe.

Well, ask and ye shall receive. One day, just after we returned from a tai chi class, the phone rang. It was a woman who had met a friend of ours, and he had given her our phone number. She was trying to find a home for a female black Lab. In about five minutes, Betsy was at our house. When I opened the door of her van, I saw two adult dogs: one looked like a German shepherd and the other was a black Lab. There were also two puppies in the car.

Betsy told me she was an ardent dog lover. The animals belonged to a young couple that lived near her. They had three preschool children and eleven dogs, and they worked full time. Betsy had told them she would try to find a home for the Lab, her litter of five puppies, and the German shepherd. She had found a home for three of the puppies that morning but still had the two adult dogs and two puppies to give away.

The Lab looked just like the dog Robert had said he wanted. However, when I approached her, she growled at me. Even when Betsy took the puppies out of the van, the Lab wouldn't come out. Meanwhile, the German shepherd wagged her tail vigorously and jumped right out. She started to run across the street, but when Betsy called, "Kelly," she immediately came back. She came up to me with her tail wagging. It was love at first sight. I thought she was adorable.

Robert was waiting inside the house in the living room. I opened the door, and Kelly walked right in, turned to the right, went down the hall past the bedrooms to the kitchen, around to the dining room, and back full circle to the living room. She jumped up on the couch next to Robert and waited for him to pet her.

I told him about the Lab and how she had reacted to me when I had tried to greet her. Robert said, "Well, the house passed her inspection. I guess Kelly has adopted us." Betsy then tried very hard to get us to take a puppy also—as a companion for Kelly—but I firmly declined.

When Betsy found out this was my first dog, she decided to stay and help me give Kelly a bath. Kelly had been an outside dog, and Betsy thought she needed to have a bath before she could lie on our light-colored couch. So I found some baby shampoo, and we gave her a bath in the bathtub.

Kelly seemed glad when it was over but had tolerated the ordeal in a good-natured way.

By the time Betsy left, I was overwhelmed. As you've probably already surmised, I'm a planner—a person who likes to be prepared for things. I'm usually good at predicting events and at anticipating the behavior of others. This allows me to be ready for whatever happens. I guess I feel I have more control of situations that way.

Well, in that hour or so, Robert and I had suddenly become adoptive parents. Usually with parenthood, you have at least a seven-month lead-time to get the nursery ready and buy supplies, clothes, toys, etc. In our case, the new arrival had been spontaneously delivered, and we had no food, no bed, and no toys—nothing. We did have a secure back yard; that was good, for a start. So, off we went to shop for our new arrival.

Kelly was probably a mix of border collie and German shepherd. Her coloring was black and tan, with some white on her belly. Her hair was long, and her tail was long and flanged like a collie's. She weighed thirty-seven pounds and was the size of a border collie—much smaller than a German shepherd. But her ears were pointed like a German shepherd's. In short, she was beautiful.

Betsy told us Kelly had had at least one litter of puppies. After we got her, we found out she was in heat. As soon as possible, we took her to the vet for shots and spaying. The vet said that, judging from her teeth, she was at least four years old.

Kelly was truly heaven-sent; we could not have found a better dog for us. It appeared someone had trained her well. She was housebroken and had phenomenal bladder control, especially when compared with her two elderly caretakers. She generally obeyed well and adapted easily to new environments and people. She was a good guard dog, barking when a stranger came to the door or into the yard. And she was very loving and lovable.

Shortly after she came to us, we renamed her Lady. The name just seemed to suit her. She would lie demurely with her front paws crossed as she watched us busily doing things. One of her favorite things was to have her belly rubbed. Once she had determined you were a friend (and most people qualified), she would lie on her back and spread her legs, hoping for a belly rub. I told Robert, "I think the Lady is a tramp."

Lady was also a companion to Robert wherever he went. When he could no longer reach down to pet her, she would stand by his chair with her head on his knee, so he could reach her better. Lady also loved, and was loved by other people who came to visit us.

Many of our family and friends from Florida came to visit us that year. It was wonderful. We were able to take them to various sites in the area, go out to eat, talk, reminisce, and enjoy quality time with them. Robert wasn't as physically active as he had been and tired more easily, but no major changes had yet occurred to interfere with his ability to enjoy interactions. We got everyone on videotape so we could replay the memories.

In September of that year, my high school class was having its fiftieth class reunion. I had moved away from my hometown after graduation, and although I went back to see family members for many years, it had never been at a reunion time. Robert encouraged me to go, and when one of my girlfriends from school invited me to stay with her, I decided I would. Robert assured me he would be all right; he had his car and his Geezer Group, and he could go out to eat part of the time. He was still self-reliant. He would stay busy tending his garden, and he had Lady to take care of. "You should go," he said. "You'll have a great time seeing everyone again." So I went. I was gone about six days and called him each day to see how he was doing.

It was good for both of us. I was able to experience a world I hadn't been part of for a long time, see those old friends, get an update on their lives, and revisit many memories of a time when life was simple and held infinite promise. It was good to focus on something other than my small corner of the world.

The time apart was good for Robert, too. He was able to feel independent and in control of his daily life. He was living on his own, and he felt reaffirmed that, although he had some impairments, he could still take care of himself, his house and garden, and his dog. He felt positive about himself and life. Yes, times were still good!

FYI Commentary

How do you cope with a terminal diagnosis?

When you receive a terminal or life-threatening diagnosis, it's vital to take advantage of whatever support groups are available—to network with others who are having similar problems. If your loved one is resistant to participating, go by yourself as the caregiver. You need the support to help you to cope with the situation and help you not feel alone and isolated. Other people can provide a wealth of information and tips for coping. Remember, if the caregiver isn't taken care of, you may end up having two patients with no caregiver.

Your doctor can probably provide you with information about how and where to contact support groups. You can also check in the Yellow Pages of your local phone book or on the Internet. The local newspaper and local radio stations often have information regarding support groups, too. Most areas have a senior center, another good source of information and assistance.

It's also important to share information with your family members and friends to keep them aware of what's happening and allow them to prepare for the worst. Both patients and caregivers need each other's support emotionally and, if possible, physically to lighten the load.

Research has shown that pets can be very therapeutic for persons experiencing debilitating changes. Pets provide patients with something to be responsible for and to focus on other than themselves. Animals can provide unconditional love and serve as a companion for both the patient and the caregiver. Be mindful of the size, activity level, and neediness of the animal you select. Some animals can put the patient at risk for falling. Some aren't conducive to rest, need too much care for the circumstances, and can be more of a problem than a blessing. So choose carefully when selecting a pet as a therapeutic measure.

Pets can be found through a local Humane Society or other animal shelter, friends, pet shops, and the Internet. Your senior center may have information on pets that need a home because their owners are moving or are entering an assisted-living facility or nursing home and can't take their pets with them.

It's important to use the time available with your loved one as wisely as you can. If there are experiences that he or she wishes to enjoy while still able, don't wait to make them happen. Seize the day! Tomorrow may be too late.

REVERSING ROLES

. . . .

As WE NEARED THE BEGINNING of 2005, Robert and I had pretty much settled into a routine. We had adapted to the changes of the past year, and things were running smoothly. Most of the changes involved adding appointments and treatments to our regular schedule. We were busier, but that wasn't a negative thing. Because we were aware that the long-term prognosis wasn't good, we were living very much in the now. We savored our experiences, such as the visits of friends and family; special days like holidays, birthdays, and anniversaries; just being together and holding hands or lying next to each other in bed. We no longer took things— or each other—for granted. We had a lot of quality time of living and loving well.

Because of Parkinson's, Robert's handwriting became so small that it was hardly legible, and it was a very slow process for him even to sign his name. He had always signed, addressed, and prepared our Christmas cards for mailing. That year, he just wasn't able to do it. So we made it a joint effort. I signed our names and addressed the envelopes; he stuffed, sealed, and stamped them. It worked well, and we both enjoyed the project.

For years, Robert had done much of the grocery shopping for the two of us. He would stop daily to pick up whatever we needed or whatever caught his eye. Once a week, we would go shopping together and get the entrée items for the next week. As he became less steady on his feet, he had to rely on the cart to navigate around the store. And as the numbness in his feet increased, he made fewer visits to the grocery store by himself.

Robert began using a quad cane to help with his balance. This type of cane balances on four short legs and has a curved handle. I had given him a hand-carved, more traditional cane for his birthday, but he preferred the quad style. A walker was helpful when he walked around the yard. We lived in desert climate, and our yard was xeriscaped. In the front and side yards were crushed rocks and stones; the back patio area was covered with stones, and the garden had sand for walkways. It wasn't level, partly because Lady loved to race around the plants and partly because, when it did rain, the water usually ran off, making deep furrows and gullies. Even with good balance, it could be difficult to walk around in our yard. With a cane or walker it was nearly impossible.

Spring moved into summer, and the numbness in Robert's feet and legs became worse. This made driving difficult because it was hard for him to judge the pressure he was applying to the gas and brake pedals. Also, he couldn't feel for sure whether his foot was on the gas pedal or the brake pedal. So he made the decision to give up driving altogether. I was relieved because his driving had been jerky for some time. He would take alternate routes to avoid a hill or sharp curve, and he drove much slower than necessary most of the time. I was afraid he would have an accident.

I became the family chauffeur. This was a total role reversal; Robert had always driven when we rode together— for over twenty years. He didn't like to be a passenger in any vehicle. If we were going out to eat with another couple, we would usually meet them at the restaurant, because he didn't want to ride with them. It was a control issue for him. If he wasn't at the wheel, he wasn't comfortable. He wouldn't ride buses, airplanes, or trains for the same reason. I was very proud of him for making that difficult decision. He did adjust to being the passenger but not without some difficulty.

In June of 2005, my sister's children planned a surprise party for their parents' fiftieth wedding anniversary. I hadn't seen my sister for four years. She was in her eighties, and we knew that it would only become more difficult for me to visit. It would be an opportunity for me to see all of my remaining relatives in my family of origin.

Robert encouraged me to go to the event, which was in Michigan. We talked about the arrangements that we would need to make since I would be gone for about five and a half days. Robert was no longer driving, so he would be homebound. He talked with his Geezer Group, and they agreed to pick him up for coffee on a couple of mornings. I made arrangements for Meals on Wheels to deliver a hot meal on weekdays. And he and another friend would go out for dinner on the weekend. I made sure the refrigerator was full and the pantry was stocked with his favorite snacks. He felt he could manage just fine, even without a car. So I went. I called him each day to see how things were going. He did just fine.

When I got home, I noticed a number of covered containers in the refrigerator. Robert told me they were part of the meals that had been delivered to the house. He said he had opened them, smelled them, and poked at them. And when he couldn't decide what they were, he just put them back in the fridge. Turns out some of the items were things he really liked but didn't recognize. For example, one container held canned apricot halves.

Now, Robert likes canned apricots. However, about six halves were packed tightly into a small container with the skin side up, so they appeared to be hard. He didn't know what they were. When I took them out of the container and put them in a sauce dish with a little juice, he ate them immediately. He said he gave many of the entrees to the dog. Nevertheless, he seemed to have managed very well while I was gone.

By midsummer, Robert had started having a great deal of pain in his legs, and the numbness in his feet worsened. Dr. Spruce told us about a new infrared treatment at the local hospital's physical therapy department that might help. The infrared rays stimulate the blood flow in the area where applied, thereby reducing the pain, promoting healing, and in Robert's case, relieving some of the numbness. She wrote us a consult, and Robert started the treatments.

The treatments were a combination of exercise on non-weight-bearing machines followed by the application of the infrared strips to his legs and feet. He felt the treatments were therapeutic, and we went three times a week for a month. We decided to buy an infrared unit for use at home once the treatments at the hospital were over. We continued doing the infrared treatments at home for several months.

In September, we received a call from Robert's daughter in Florida. She was in the hospital and needed to arrange to have a caregiver in her home before they would discharge her. I was the only one she had who might be able to do that for her. Robert and I talked it over, and we decided I should go.

I got a medical-status airplane ticket and left as soon as I could make all the arrangements. Robert didn't want Meals on Wheels. My sister-in-law came over each day to apply the infrared strips to Robert's feet and legs. She also got him any groceries he needed, and they went out to dinner a couple of times. I was gone for ten days, and I called him every day to see how he was getting along. Again he seemed to manage well during my absence.

By late summer of 2005, Robert was able to do less and less work in the yard. Keeping up our yard was a full-time job during some parts of the year. Unlike the popular song, Robert had promised me a rose garden before we were married, and he had tried to grow roses for me in Florida. But his attempts were not very successful, because the ground was too acidic.

When we moved to New Mexico, he found that roses would grow well there. He planted over fifty rose bushes in the yard, and his garden was his pride and joy. He loved bringing me bouquets of roses from our yard. The yard was *his* hobby, and I didn't interfere with it. So when he became too unsteady on his feet (even with the walker) to prune, fertilize, and weed the garden, I became the designated gardener, and he became the adviser/consultant. He taught me how to take care of the yard: how to prune, when to fertilize, how to prepare wells for water retention, how and when to apply mulch and chips, and of course how to keep the weed population at bay.

During this time, he continued to take his medications, complete his exercises as prescribed, cooperate, and be helpful as his circumstances allowed. I never heard him complain, act as if he felt sorry for himself, or get angry because of his situation. Nor was he depressed. The only way I learned about his pain was through observation and by asking him, in typical nurse fashion, if he had any pain. He seemed to accept the changes that were happening to him.

I tried to roll with the punches, to make things work as best I could. If he was no longer able to do something, and it had to be done, I took it on. I had always been healthy and active, so I was just being more so. What I didn't realize—until right now—was the extent of the lifestyle changes he was experiencing and all the roles he had to surrender to someone else. A good many of the activities that had provided pleasure and added pride to his life were no longer available to him. Although I wasn't seeing it, the quality of his life was diminishing before my very eyes.

FYI Commentary

Our town's senior center has two si
available to seniors. They serve break.
weekday for a nominal fee: seventy-five cents for
and $1.50 for the noon meal. Breakfast consists of a variety
of egg dishes, sausage and bacon, potatoes, toast, hot and
cold cereals, pancakes, and assorted beverages. Noon meal
includes an entrée, hot vegetable, potato, rice or pasta dish,
salad, rolls, beverage, and dessert. If you're homebound, you
can call and arrange to have your meals delivered. Breakfast
is a sack meal of cereal, milk, and fruit that arrives along
with the noon meal, which is delivered hot. Weekend meals
are delivered on Friday and are frozen versions of the usual
noon hot meal.

This is a wonderful service for seniors who are on a
limited budget, have difficulty grocery shopping, or can't
prepare meals. The meal sites also provide socialization for
people who might otherwise be isolated or spending most of
their time alone.

Check your Yellow Pages or the Internet for the location
of senior centers in your area, and inquire about the services
and activities available. Usually they have a wide range of
options to choose from.

RAPIDLY OCCURRING CHANGES

···

IF I WERE TO DESCRIBE the first nine months of 2005, I would label them "the calm before the storm." The month of October seemed to be the turning point. Everything became more difficult for Robert. When we talked to the neurologist about this, he decided to increase the dosage of Robert's Parkinson's medications to see if more medication would result in less debilitation.

Robert went from the quad cane to a rolling walker (a walker with four wheels). He pushed it in front of him for stability, and it had a seat that he could sit on if he needed to stop and rest while ambulating/walking from one place to another. It also had a storage unit under the seat to keep needed items close at hand. Robert found the walker very handy around the house.

I had seen one of these walkers advertised in a medical supply catalog we received in the mail. Also, some friends had a standard walker that had been used by a relative who was recovering from a broken hip. It was stored in their garage, and they brought it over for Robert to use. It was the classic style of walker used for rehab patients. It folded easily and was lightweight. Robert used it when we went out in the car (such as to his Geezer Group or a restaurant).

It became very hard for Robert to get up from the sofa or a chair—and even from the commode. So we got a raised toilet seat. Eventually, we got a lift chair. A lift or tilt chair has a remote-control device that lifts the chair seat forward and up to a convenient height for the user, making it easier to sit down and get up. It also functions as a recliner. It became a favorite place for Robert to nap in the afternoon and often served as a bed on nights when his legs were unusually painful.

I also bought him a shower chair, because he was afraid that he might fall in the shower. I ordered the most compact style of chair I could find. However, the walk-in shower was small, and Robert was a big man—five foot eleven, 260 pounds, and with a very large frame. There just wasn't enough room for him and the chair in the shower together. So he began bathing less often.

Working the daily crossword puzzle had always been one of Robert's hobbies. It was like a mental check and reality monitor for him. Completing the puzzle confirmed that both his mind and his body were still working properly. However, now he was able to complete less and less of it. His printing had become so tiny that even he couldn't make out what he put in the blanks. Also, he was having increased problems with working the puzzle itself. Answers that he used to know would no longer come to him.

I called Dr. Spruce to report these changes. She suggested that I find a home health aide to assist Robert with bathing and personal care. The agency nurse came to the house, and we filled out the necessary paperwork. We decided that a wheelchair would probably be helpful for when he had to go any distance, such as to his appointment with the neurologist on the second floor of the hospital.

The first time the home health aides came to give Robert a shower, we discovered how non-user friendly our main bathroom was for a handicapped person. The wheelchair would not go through the doorway. The tub/shower area was so small that two large people could hardly be in it at one time. Having Robert and his aide and the rolling walker together in that small area made showering a real challenge.

The shower chair I'd purchased wasn't feasible because Robert could no longer step into the tub to take a shower. The aide brought a sliding tub transfer bench that he could sit down on outside the tub. Then, with the assistance of the aide, he could swing his legs inside, and the seat area would slide until he was sitting in the shower area. This was a very helpful piece of equipment. We also realized there were no handrails to hold onto for safety and stabilization. The bathroom definitely needed a makeover.

As fate would have it, Robert and I were already planning to have our living room enlarged. We had made the plans early that summer and had decided to delay the start of the project until after Labor Day, because my daughter was coming to visit that weekend. The project included extending the front wall of the house out to incorporate a porch area into the living room. It would triple the window area and enlarge the room by about ninety square feet. We felt it would enhance our living space and make a more comfortable area for entertaining guests.

We had also decided not to start the project until fall because of the need for air-conditioning in New Mexico during the summer months. We planned that it would be finished well before Christmas. These plans were already in progress before Robert's functional decline escalated. When we realized the difficulty the bathroom area was presenting, we changed the plan to include remodeling of the bathroom before making any alteration to the living room. The base for the extension and the new sidewalk areas had been started in late September. At the end of October, we shifted gears; the bathroom area became the priority.

Robert's study was in the room next to the bathroom. It was a corner room and had been designed as a bedroom. Along the interior wall was a double closet that extended into the bathroom. We had it taken out to enlarge the bathroom area. With the closet gone, we could get a wheelchair through the bathroom door and had plenty of room for bathing, dressing, etc. This also made the bathroom accessible from the adjoining room. It was finished by Thanksgiving and was much more convenient for Robert and for his caregivers.

Robert and I had previously discussed our wishes about end-of-life decisions. We wanted to remain at home and have home hospice care rather than hospitalization. Parkinson's is a terminal disease that usually progresses very slowly. However, Robert's condition suddenly seemed to be like a wildfire out of control. I decided that I would make the study into Robert's bedroom once he became bed-bound. It had wonderful morning sun and was a large, pleasant room.

With access directly to the bathroom, it would be like a suite of rooms just for Robert and his care.

By the first of December, his activity level had declined greatly. It was more difficult for him to ambulate, to sit and stand, and to transfer from one area to another. He tired more easily too. Dr. Spruce felt that physical therapy would be helpful for maintaining his muscle strength and mobility.

Lewis, the physical therapist, came to the house twice a week for about forty-five minutes to help Robert ambulate and exercise. The home health aide, Dave, came three mornings a week for an hour. He would assist Robert in getting out of bed, showering, shaving, and dressing. A nurse made a visit once a week for about fifteen minutes to assess changes and to see if we needed additional equipment, assistance, or information. It was usually a different nurse each visit.

Robert could no longer ambulate without assistance. He frequently had diarrhea and was often incontinent. He just couldn't react quickly enough to get to the bathroom in time. I guess I should say "we." He could no longer get to the bathroom by himself.

He also had increased urgency with urination. During the day, we would hang a urinal on the side of his walker, so it would be readily available. But he couldn't use it while sitting down. Therefore, he needed assistance to stand up, and he needed both of his hands to hold on to the walker for balance while standing up. So he needed assistance holding the urinal. At night, he was up about every two hours to urinate and needed that assistance. Accidents were becoming more frequent, so I bought him pull-ups to wear for both day and night to protect his clothing and the furniture.

I was fearful of leaving Robert alone, because he needed such frequent assistance. My sister-in-law would have been more than willing to sit with him, but she didn't feel comfortable assisting him with toileting. I very much needed time to run errands and shop.

Finally, I heard about respite care provided by the senior center. An aide could come to the house and care for Robert once a week for as long as four hours. I called and made the arrangements. Janet began coming to be with Robert one morning a week. I could have four hours away from the house—time to do whatever I needed to do. Oh, I felt the universe had sent me an angel! Janet and Robert got along well. They would sing, watch a video, or listen to CDs. She would fix him a cup of coffee or a snack if he wanted one. She would toilet him, if needed. They enjoyed their time together.

I enjoyed my time apart, too. It was wonderful. Usually I would hurry and do my errands and grocery shopping. Then I would meet my sister-in-law for coffee and a scone at a small café downtown. I would vent; she would update me on our friends from the line-dancing group; we would visit with the café owners and other patrons we knew; and we would just have plain girl talk. I usually had about two hours to spend over coffee, and it was *so* therapeutic. I looked forward to those two hours every week—somewhat like a child awaits Christmas.

I felt like I was running on pure adrenalin. I was up so frequently during the night with Robert that I wasn't getting enough rest, and my days were filled with the constant activities involving his care. I was also trying to get the Christmas cards sent out and gifts ready to mail to the children, and I wanted to make the living room festive for Christmas.

However, I didn't do much decorating. Time was limited, space was limited because of Robert's additional assistive devices, and my energy was limited. I did decorate the mantel with a lighted garland and put up the Christmas tree. We had always loved celebrating Christmas—decorating the house and yard, sending cards and gifts, having friends and family over, etc. I felt this might be the last Christmas Robert and I would enjoy together, and I wanted it to be as pleasant a memory as possible.

About two weeks into December, I called Dr. Spruce and told her I thought we needed a hospital bed, an over-the-bed table, and a bedside commode. It was so difficult for me to give Robert a bed bath and dress him while he lay in our king-sized bed. My former idea about using the front room off the remodeled bathroom for his bedroom had to be scrapped. It would have entailed moving a desk, four bookcases, a piano, and other pieces of furniture out of that room and into the guest bedroom. Then the furniture in the guest room would need to be moved to the front room. I didn't have the time, the energy, or the manpower available to get that job done. So I got a friend to help me move the double bed out of the guest room into storage. The guest bedroom was next to the master bedroom, and I felt it would be more convenient for me if he were in the adjoining room.

The hospital bed, table, and commode arrived, and we got them set up. I had to go to the store and buy sheets and other linen for the hospital bed. I also decided to get a baby monitor so I could hear Robert better from the master bedroom when he called to me during the night.

The hospital bed did make bathing and dressing Robert and changing the bed linens easier. I usually had to change the linens every morning, but I also had to change the pads and Robert's pull-ups at least once during the night. The pull-ups just didn't hold all the urine output, even when reinforced with an extra pad.

Also, when Robert felt the urge to urinate, he would get restless and try to climb out of the bed. I was afraid he would hurt himself in the attempt. So every time I heard him stir, I would get up to check on him. I was up about every two hours throughout the night.

I talked frequently with the children and our friends. There's a two-hour time difference between New Mexico and Florida, so when they called, I was often in the middle of assisting Robert. We decided on a phone chain: one of the kids would call and talk to us, and then relay the conversation to one of the others, and that person would call someone else, etc. A different child would start the chain each time, so we all got to talk to each one periodically.

I kept them aware of the changes that were occurring, because I didn't want them to have any surprises. They were very concerned about both of us and tried to be as supportive as possible. They always inquired about how I was holding up, if I was getting enough sleep, if I was getting enough help. When it became obvious to them that the answer to the first question was "Barely" and the answers to the last two questions were "No," they posed these questions to me: "Don't you think the situation is becoming too much for you to handle? Have you thought about putting Robert in a nursing home?"

I didn't want to think about those questions. I had promised Robert I would care for him at home. I told him that, after all, I was a nurse, and I could do his bedside nursing care. However, I had to remind myself that a nurse doesn't work 24/7. A nurse generally works a maximum of a twelve-hour shift, and then another nurse comes on duty to relieve her. I was realizing that his care was becoming overwhelming for me, but I still didn't want him to go into a nursing home. I had promised I wouldn't do that to him. The situation was a real dilemma for me.

Several friends told me that if he went into a nursing home, we would lose all our savings and our house—everything—to pay for the care, and then we would both have to go on Medicaid. I heard so much conflicting information, none of which I liked, that I finally decided to call the local Medicaid agency for their input. They suggested that I make an appointment to come to the office and talk with them. So I made an appointment for the next time that Janet was to come and sit with Robert. I felt it might be a long interview.

Later that week, I kept the appointment. The man was very nice and very informative. I didn't like hearing what he told me, but I needed to hear it so I could separate fact from myth. He gave me a packet of information I could read at home and an application to apply for financial assistance. He told me that when I had made a decision and was ready to proceed, I should make another appointment. I didn't tell Robert about the interview or what I had learned.

Robert seemed to accept his rapid decline well. He didn't complain. He was very compliant with whatever he was told to do. But he could do less and less. He also seemed to comprehend less and less. It was as though his mind was in a fog, and his body wouldn't readily respond for him. He would try, but he just couldn't seem to make his body or his mind work properly.

I was becoming a basket case. I was chronically tired, and his care had become even more strenuous because he wasn't able to help very much. I'm about 127 pounds and only five three. He was like dead weight, and his 260-pound body was impossible for me to transfer.

I was often frustrated by the situation, but I had no one there to help me. I would get irritable, and then I would yell at him. It didn't help, because he didn't seem to understand why I was getting upset. Then I would feel guilty for yelling at him. After all, he was trying his best, and it wasn't his fault that he couldn't do any better.

I felt like a failure as a nurse; nurses don't yell at their patients, no matter how frustrated they might be. I felt like a failure as a wife, particularly when I thought about having to put Robert in a nursing home. I felt like I was betraying my best friend, selling out my soul mate. I also was fearful of having to give up all our savings so we could qualify for Medicaid. There were no good options.

Robert went to bed at about eight o'clock, and I usually stayed up until nine or ten, often talking with the kids. It was my only quiet time of the day. It gave me a time to unwind and rest my body before trying to go to sleep. During these times, my doubts and guilt would surface. I felt so inadequate, so alone, and so helpless—and I felt there was nowhere to turn for help.

FYI Commentary

Where can you get medical equipment and supplies?

As your loved ones begin to lose their ability to function, medical equipment and supplies can be helpful in extending their independence and quality of life. Health care aids can be found in multiple places. If you live in a larger city, there is likely a medical supply store where you can select and purchase home health aids and equipment. Often drugstores sell a variety of assistive devices. The Yellow Pages of your local phone book probably list the places in your community that sell or rent the items you're looking for. If you live in a very small town, as I do, you may find mail-order catalogs an efficient way to have items delivered to your door. Or you may want to use the Internet to find and purchase what you need.

Ask your doctor or nurse for information about places to find supplies and equipment. And be sure to check with a senior center. They sometimes lend equipment that has been donated to them. When you no longer need it, you return the device and then it's lent to someone else who can use it.

The list of items you might find helpful is endless. After looking through a catalog or a medical supply store, you may find items that you didn't realize existed. Often they can make your life so much easier as well as improve your loved one's quality of life.

What services can a home health agency provide, and how can you make home health care available to your loved one?

To use the services of a home health agency, you'll need a referral from the patient's doctor. The usual procedure starts with the doctor's referral to the agency followed by a visit from a home health nurse. He or she will come to the patient's home and interview both the patient and the caregiver, if there is one present. Often the patient/client lives alone, and there's no regular caregiver available. The nurse assesses the client's needs and the home environment to see what services will best serve the client. He or she will talk with the client and the caregiver(s) regarding suggestions, and together they'll develop a tentative plan for providing assistance in the home. This may include bathing, dressing, grooming, shaving, exercising, eating, or completing other daily activities. An evaluation of the safety of the environment may also be done. Services will vary, depending on the client's circumstances and environment.

Members of a home health agency work in teams, which usually include nurses, nursing assistants or aides, physical therapists, and occupational therapists. The team, headed by the nurse, works with the doctor to closely monitor care and changes in the client's status. Usually private insurance, Medicare, and/or Medicaid cover all or part of the costs for the services.

Home health agencies often provide or make arrangements for necessary equipment for the client. Equipment, including oxygen service, is often covered by insurance and is usually rented.

What changes will you need to better care for your loved one in your home?

As the needs of your loved one increase because of debilitation, the home environment will need to be altered. As needed equipment is added, space must be found both for its use and its storage. It may be necessary to rearrange furniture and alter the purpose of a certain room. Patient comfort and convenience become the priority. Caregiver efficiency and energy conservation are important too, as is the safety of both the patient and the caregiver.

Safety begins with fall prevention. Make clear pathways to the bathroom, in the kitchen, to the bedroom, and in all major living areas. Remove throw rugs and small furniture or objects that might cause one to trip. Areas should have sufficient lighting to prevent running into or tripping over objects. Night-lights can be very helpful, especially for caregivers. For patients who have impaired use of their hands, changing door handles, light switches, and faucet handles can increase and prolong independence.

Handrails and grab bars should be placed in strategic areas. Foam cushions and extra padding may increase patient comfort. In bathrooms, handheld showerheads, shower chairs or benches, raised toilet seats, grab bars, etc., are important for safety and convenience. Canes, walkers, transport chairs, wheelchairs, and wheelchair ramps may be needed. And the list goes on.

The assistive devices and equipment needed vary with each patient's diagnoses, age, and individual circumstances and resources. However, it's vitally important for the patient, family members, and caregivers to be aware of basic safety issues and fall prevention measures. Falls and other accidents often result in complications more serious than the patient's original health issues. Often a simple fall will lead to increased discomfort, debilitation, and complications that become fatal.

What is respite care?

You've probably heard the saying, "Never kill the goose that lays the golden eggs." It applies very well to caregivers, who are an important consideration in treatment planning. If a caregiver wears out or burns out, he or she can no longer function sufficiently to care for the patient, and you may soon have two persons needing care.

There are no gold medals for playing the martyr. If you are a caregiver, make your needs a priority, or soon you won't be able to meet the needs of your patient. Ask for help wherever it may be available. This includes asking for the equipment and supplies that make your job easier and safer. It also includes asking friends, neighbors, and family members to help where and when they can.

Also remember that the job you're doing may not always be perfect, but life isn't perfect. "Do the best you can with what you have to work with, and be satisfied" was Robert's favorite saying. You can't do better than your best, and there's no room in the equation for guilt.

If you have home health services in your area, ask them about respite care. And ask them if they have suggestions regarding additional resources. If you doubt yourself regarding the care you're able to provide, talk with the nurse on the team. He or she may be able to point out shortcuts or more effective ways to get the job done and may help you prioritize what needs to be done. Reach out for help to conserve your health as much as possible. That will enable you to provide better care for your loved one and to be there for him or her for a longer time.

TURNING POINT

. . . .

IT WAS ABOUT A WEEK before Christmas, a Sunday. I had to
keep reminding myself what day it was. Each day seemed
to morph into the next, and the only landmarks for me were
visits from Dave, Robert's aide, and Lewis, his physical
therapist.

Robert's appetite was waning. I could tell he was hungry,
but he said nothing tasted good; he complained that everything
had a metallic taste. He had diarrhea almost daily, and I felt
sure he was losing weight. He was very anxious and restless,
day and night. He seemed confused at times, and it was
very difficult for him to follow directions. His tremors were
more pronounced. I gave him liquids in a Sippy cup, and at
mealtimes I had to feed him everything he ate.

I remember that Thursday, December 22, very well—
only three days until Christmas. It had been a difficult day.
Lewis had come and tried to have Robert ambulate outside

for a short bit, so he could get some fresh air. He was having him try to walk down the concrete driveway and back. Lewis was assisting Robert with a gait belt for safety. However, Robert also asked me to follow closely behind them with the wheelchair—just in case he couldn't continue. He could only make it about six feet when he began to waiver. We eased him into the wheelchair and returned to the house.

That evening, I decided I would try to create an ambience that would help us both relax and maybe capture a bit of the holiday spirit. I lit some candles, lit the gas log, and turned on the Christmas tree lights and the lights on the mantel. I also put on a CD of our favorite Christmas music. We sat together on the couch with Lady at our feet. Robert had his head in my lap. We talked of Christmases past—or maybe I should say I talked and Robert mostly listened. But he seemed to enjoy the moment. It was relaxing to both of us.

However, it wasn't very long before he became restless and wanted to go to bed. I helped him into his wheelchair and wheeled him to his bedroom. Then I positioned the wheelchair to help him transfer to the bed. He seemed very confused. Instead of the usual transfer, he attempted to get into bed with his hands and chest first. But then he couldn't lift his legs to get the lower half of his body into the bed. And I couldn't get him turned around or back into the wheelchair.

Robert lowered himself to the floor and was kneeling beside the bed as one would to say his prayers. I didn't know what to do. I couldn't help him. He finally decided he would just sleep on the floor. Of course, this was not an acceptable option to me, so I called our next-door neighbor to ask for help. No one was available.

So I called our neighbor across the street from us. Dan is a tall, athletic man in his early fifties and was always willing to help if he could. He and his wife came over, and we finally got Robert off the floor and into the bed. But it was a difficult job even for Dan. Robert tried to help. However, he was so confused, he just wasn't able to. He was 250-plus pounds of dead weight. As Dan and his wife left, they urged me to call if I needed any further help. I thanked them both, and once they were gone, I got Robert changed for bed and settled for sleep.

When I was finished, I returned to the living room. I turned on the baby monitor so I would hear Robert if he stirred. I could already hear his measured breathing; he was asleep.

I sat down in the recliner. The room had a warm glow from the candles, the fire, and the Christmas lights. Lady lay in her bed by the fire and looked up at me. I just sat very, very still for quite some time. Then a deep feeling of aloneness came over me. I could feel Robert fading from me. He was physically in the other room, but that was primarily his body. His essence, his spirit, was fading fast. I was losing him—the part of him that could communicate with me and respond to me. That part of him was ebbing away before my very eyes.

I got down on the floor and knelt by Lady. I put my arms around her and hugged her. Suddenly, I uttered a deep, heart-rending sob from the bowels of my soul, then another, and another. Finally, the tears flowed—in torrents. Lady just lay there quietly, letting me hold her.

I knew the Robert I had lived with for the last twenty-four years would never be there with me again. I had lost touch with my soul mate. My best friend was gone to me. I could still care for his body, but it was like the empty shell of the man I loved.

Once the sobbing stopped and the tears were spent, I turned off the fire log and the lights, hugged the dog one more time, and headed for my bed. I picked up the monitor and, on the way to my bedroom, stopped to kiss Robert goodnight. I felt so alone and so empty.

FYI Commentary

The importance of asking for and receiving help

It has always been difficult for me to ask for help. Maybe it's too much ego on my part; it means admitting my limitations, or perhaps more honestly, it makes me feel inadequate to admit that I need help and to ask for it. Many caregivers experience feelings of guilt and frustration because of their inability to provide all the care needed at certain times.

Nurses are trained to recognize the need for additional assistance and call for backup in difficult situations. They know that a team effort is often required to ensure a patient's health and safety. Recognizing the situations that require additional assistance indicates good judgment on the part of a nurse.

There are limits to what one individual can do alone. I was a care giving wife, not a nurse, during much of the time of Robert's illness. Remembering to call for backup from friends, neighbors, and family is an important aspect of being a caregiver. Most people want to help and often feel honored to assist when a person is in need. As the saying goes, "It is more blessed to give than to receive," but for every giver, there also has to be a receiver. It's equally as important to allow others to give to you as it is for you to give to others. There's a time for all things, and it's important for *caregivers* to also allow themselves to be *care receivers*. This lesson was difficult for me to learn, but necessity forced me to become better at it.

Do you often feel separated from your loved one?

As your loved one's illness and debilitation progresses, there will likely be a point at which the person loses the ability to communicate and interact with you or other family members in a qualitative way. The mind seems to withdraw, and the center of its focus becomes the needs of the failing body. When this happens, it 's usually very difficult for the caregiver. You may feel shut out, alone, unappreciated, and disconnected from your loved one. It's important to realize that your feelings are valid and normal in the process of caring for someone with a debilitating, chronic, and/or terminal illness.

Joining a support group early in the process may help you to prepare for this time. Sharing experiences and feelings in a group setting can help you to become aware of what may happen and to accept that it is a part of the disease process and that you are unable to change the course of events.

Allowing your feelings to surface and expressing them (such as through venting, crying, or praying) will be therapeutic for you and allow you to pick up the pieces and go on. It is not a sign of weakness or failure, but a way of regenerating the spirit. Keeping your feelings pent up inside, being brave, and not showing your emotions are formulas for becoming a walking time bomb that could explode. You could lose it anytime and anywhere. As the saying goes, "Let go and let God."

HOME ALONE

· ·

DAVE CAME THE NEXT MORNING, Friday, to help Robert shower, shave, and get ready for the day. He reminded me that it would be a long holiday weekend and he wouldn't be coming again until the following Tuesday. I thought, *Indeed, it will be a long weekend.* As he left, I wished him a Merry Christmas and gave him some brownies I had baked.

Later that morning, I called Dr. Spruce's office to update her on Robert's status. The office girl told me Dr. Spruce would be out of the office for the Christmas holidays, but she would be back to see patients the following Tuesday. As I hung up the phone, I thought again, *Yes, it's going to be a* very *long weekend.*

The day was busy with the usual routine. Robert's care and the other household chores made the time pass quickly. His status was pretty much the same as it had been the last few days: agitation, confusion, decreased appetite, diarrhea, and decreased functional abilities. He also seemed to tire more easily. I felt that he might be dying. I took his vital signs, and they were within normal limits. That was encouraging, but it was puzzling to me that his general level of function had declined so rapidly. Usually, the decline in Parkinson's disorder is much slower.

Saturday was Christmas Eve. We had always celebrated Christmas on the evening of December 24. That year, the presents from the kids were under the tree, and we opened them together that evening. I fixed some hot chocolate, and we enjoyed it along with some Christmas cookies. Robert was diabetic, but at that point, his appetite was so poor that anything he ate was a plus.

His attention span was also short, and therefore so was our celebration. Early in the evening, he wanted to go to bed. Once he was settled and asleep, I took a long, hot shower and then went to bed myself. I was tired and feeling like saying, "Christmas? Bah humbug!"

Sunday morning, Christmas Day, was bedside care as usual. I got Robert bathed, dressed, and up in his wheelchair. I decided I would feed him first and then get myself dressed for the day—maybe in something festive for Christmas. I was preparing breakfast when Robert had to go to the bathroom.

As I was transferring him to the commode, he couldn't hold it any longer. I was definitely up close and personal at the time. Suddenly I was covered from the knees down with diarrhea—my robe, my gown, my slippers, my legs, and my feet. The floor was also covered. And, of course, so was Robert. Everything from the waist down had to be changed and washed, including his sneakers.

Once he was cleaned up and back in his wheelchair, I changed my clothes. Everything needed to be washed. Once I was dressed—in something *not* festive—I began to clean up the bathroom floor. As I was mopping it, I thought to myself, *Merry Christmas, Lee! And God help us—every one!*

When I could again turn my attention to breakfast, I fed Robert some oatmeal with milk. He seemed hungry and ate the entire bowlful of cereal Then I gave him his morning medications. As I was clearing the breakfast dishes from the table, he said he was going to throw up. Before I could get a bucket or pan to him, he vomited his medications and his cereal all over himself and the table. Again I began to clean up Robert and the area.

And suddenly, it was as though a light bulb went on in my head. *He's toxic! He's toxic from his medications!*

It was a textbook case. I once had a patient while I was working as a nurse on the in-patient psych unit with the same profile. It was finally determined that the patient was toxic on lithium. It all fit: the signs and symptoms that Robert had displayed over the last week or two: the diarrhea, the confusion, the agitation, the decreased appetite with complaints of food having a metallic taste, the difficulty with ambulation, and now the vomiting. Yes, Robert was toxic from lithium, his medication for his bipolar disorder.

I thanked God for blessing me with this insight. However, I reminded myself that I was a nurse, not a doctor. Therefore I didn't have the clout to admit a patient to the hospital (or to even diagnose, for that matter). But at least I could start to reverse the situation—to remove the contributing factors and push fluids.

I felt a ray of hope for Robert's condition. If I was right, and I felt sure I was, he wasn't dying. Lithium toxicity is reversible, and once his system was cleared of the drug, he might regain most of his ability to function, both mentally and physically. Yes! There was hope. I had hope! Well, isn't that what Christmas is supposedly all about? And a very Merry Christmas to everyone!

I tried to call the home health nurse. I got a voicemail recording, and I left a message asking her to call me as soon as possible. I said it was an emergency. I got no response. Later that day, I called again, and I got the voicemail and left another message. There was still no response.

The standard treatment for lithium toxicity is to stop the medication and hydrate the patient to flush the lithium from the body. So I started to push fluids with Robert: water, coffee, tea, and any kind of fluid I could get him to drink. I also stopped the lithium and his medications for Parkinson's and diabetes. I knew his symptoms were being caused by the interactions of those medications.

Monday came; it was the legal Christmas holiday, and again, no one would be working. It looked like we were home alone for another day. It doesn't pay to be sick during the holidays. Everything is put on hold; everything except a patient's condition. That continues or progresses without any notice of holidays or vacation times.

I called the home health nurse again that morning, but to no avail. The only voice I heard was that of the answering machine with its usual instructions. I withheld Robert's medications, and I encouraged him to drink anything he would swallow and to drink as often as possible. He hadn't had any more vomiting, and the diarrhea was less frequent. Robert was still very restless, but at least I felt I understood why.

That afternoon he decided he wanted to lie on our king-size bed to rest. The bed was lower than his hospital bed, and it would be very difficult for him to get on and off or to change positions while he was on it. I finally put a plastic drop cloth on the bed first. Once he was lying on that, I could pull on the plastic to position him more safely and comfortably on the bed. It worked well. However, it wouldn't help him to transfer back into the wheelchair. I didn't know how I was going to manage that.

While we were lying on the bed, the doorbell rang. When I answered the door, there was Lewis, the physical therapist. He explained that he had opted to work Monday as usual and had come to assist with Robert's exercise routine. I told him what had happened since the previous Thursday when he had last visited us, and I told him about my suspicion that Robert was toxic. I also complained about my repeated failed attempts to reach the nurse through the answering service.

Lewis was privy to the private phone number of the nurse on call for the weekend. He called her and left a message for her to call him. She was supposed to be available 24/7 to respond at any time of day or night when called. Lewis waited a short time for her response, but there was none. He called again and left another message, asking her to call me as soon as possible. He said it was an emergency.

It seemed futile to try to exercise Robert, but Lewis stayed for a while to talk with me. He knew I was feeling very anxious, frustrated, and tired. Before he left that afternoon, he told me that if I didn't hear from the nurse by seven that evening, I should call him. He would come to the house, help me get Robert into the car, and accompany us to the hospital emergency room.

At seven o'clock, I called Lewis, and he came. We got Robert into our car, and Lewis followed us to the hospital in his car. He helped me get Robert into the ER and then moved my car to a better long-term parking area. I couldn't have managed to do any of that by myself. I will be forever grateful for Lewis and all of his help.

I got Robert admitted to the ER and told the staff my suspicions regarding his condition. They drew blood for general lab work and for a lithium level. At our hospital, they don't process blood locally for anything but the most common tests, so it was necessary to send out the blood to test for lithium. We would have to wait up to seventy-two hours. However, they decided he was dehydrated, and they infused him with saline solution. This process lasted several hours. When completed, the hospital ER aides helped me get Robert back into the car.

When I got home, I realized I needed help to get Robert out of the car and into the house. It was past midnight, but our neighbor directly across the street had a light burning. I telephoned Jim for help. He and his wife came over and helped me get Robert into the wheelchair and into the house. Robert was somewhat brighter than he had been earlier in the day. The saline had helped to dilute some of the lithium in his system.

The next day was Tuesday. Dave came to assist Robert in getting cleaned up and ready for the day. I didn't call Dr. Spruce. She would want to get the lab results before proceeding with treatment, and they wouldn't be available until Wednesday or Thursday. So everything was on hold for another day or so. I wasn't happy about this, but I knew what the protocol was, and there didn't seem to be much choice but to be patient and wait. I didn't bother to call the home health agency again. I was angry about their inefficiency and lack of good nursing practice.

Wednesday morning at six, I was awakened by the telephone. It was the hospital ER nurse. She had just received Robert's lab results; they had processed the blood as a STAT order. The report showed his lithium level was so high that it was considered a medical emergency. She added that she would contact Dr. Spruce immediately.

Later, when Dr. Spruce called, she said she was trying to arrange to have Robert admitted to the hospital, but they had no beds available. They thought there would be a discharge early that afternoon. She called again in the afternoon and said we should take Robert to the ER, where they would start hydration therapy. There were no beds locally, and they would have to arrange a transfer for him to another hospital in another city. My neighbor Jim helped me take him to the hospital ER.

Finally, at about ten that evening, the arrangements were made to take Robert by ambulance to Albuquerque, about 175 miles north of us. There was a bed for him on the medical-surgical floor at the VA hospital.

The ambulance crew strapped Robert to the gurney. I kissed him good-bye and watched as they loaded him into the ambulance and drove away. I loaded his wheelchair into the car and drove myself home. Now I really was home alone.

FYI Commentary

What about the quality of care available over the holiday weekend?

My feelings are conflicted regarding the health care system and its lack of support during holidays—especially around Christmas. It's impossible to separate my thoughts and feelings as a professional caregiver from those of a wife and caretaker—a caretaker who was tired and frustrated and trying to cope but finding herself alone in an overwhelming situation. At the time, I was just trying to get through it and had no time to reflect on how I was feeling. That was possibly a good thing. Having no time to reflect did help me to cope with the immediate issues at hand rather than dwell on the anger I might have felt.

Looking at the situation from my current perspective and as a health care professional, I'm aware of the shortcomings of our complex health care system, whose goals aren't always met. There are big gaps in the health care delivery system. Care providers aren't all equal; there are wide differences in their competency and expertise, and therefore also the care given to patients. Some fall short of good-practice standards, and some don't always act responsibly. This is inexcusable but a reality. Communication is often incomplete between providers, and complications go undetected and misdiagnosed until they result in an emergency situation.

I've asked myself many what-if questions regarding Robert's care. I'll never know the answers to those questions. They're similar to speculations on "the road not taken." In a perfect world, many of the events in my story would have turned out differently. Of that I'm sure. But our lives in this world aren't perfect, and the world's component parts aren't perfect either. Most health care providers are dedicated and responsible persons who attempt to deliver the best care possible to their patients.

I do remain forever grateful for people like Louis, Dave, and the ER nurse, who were so supportive and caring during those days and went beyond their duty to assist in Robert's and my well-being.

THROUGH THE VALLEY
OF THE SHADOW

· ·

ON THURSDAY MORNING, I AWOKE to the sound of the telephone ringing. I looked at the clock. It was eleven. I had been so tired the night before when I came home from the hospital that I decided not to set the alarm. Robert was in good hands, and there was nothing I could do for him until I heard from his doctor.

The call was from Dr. Chan from the medical-surgery unit at the hospital. Robert had been unable to give them a medical history upon admission. I explained I was a retired psychiatric clinical nurse specialist for the VA and that Robert and I had been married for twenty-four years. I answered his questions, and he was able to complete the admission forms. I told him about Robert's physical decline in the last three months and the recent history of signs and symptoms that led to the diagnosis of lithium toxicity. We talked about Robert's former behavior and mental status.

Dr. Chan was trying to get an idea of what Robert's baseline level of function had been prior to the onset of overmedication. He told me that Robert was semi comatose, and they were attempting to bring his lithium levels down to an acceptable range. They were hoping that once the levels dropped, he would become alert and oriented again. We discussed Robert's living will choices—that he wanted no CPR or extraordinary health measures to prolong life if he were to be deemed terminal.

I informed Dr. Chan that I had no way to get to the hospital until the weekend. He assured me he would keep me informed regarding Robert's condition and told me how I could contact him if necessary. He said he would call me the next day to share any changes in Robert's condition. I thanked him for his concern and for the update.

I was familiar with how the VA system usually worked. I felt Robert would get the care he needed and, in his present condition, would not be aware of my absence. In several days, once his condition had stabilized, he would be aware of visitors and be able to participate in and better enjoy interactions.

Given the events of the last couple of weeks—not to mention months—I didn't feel competent to drive the over two-hour trip to the hospital by myself. My sister-in-law, Charline, was out of town for the Christmas holiday but would be returning the next day, Friday. I felt sure she would make the trip with me.

For the first time in a very long time, I was allowing myself to feel the extent of my fatigue. It had been so long since I'd had a complete night's sleep and so long since I hadn't been almost totally focused on Robert's care. I told myself that the next few days were reserved for *my* care and for recharging my battery. That would help me to face the days ahead with a healthier and more positive attitude.

After I hung up, I thought about my conversation with Dr. Chan. Because I was an RN and a former psych nurse, there was a certain rapport that had developed between us. We had communicated as colleagues, so the sharing of information was more doctor to nurse than doctor to patient's wife. Again I felt fortunate to be a nurse, but I wondered how I would be feeling if that had not been my background.

When Charline returned, we decided to make the trip on Sunday, the first of January. We felt the traffic would be minimal, because Monday was the legal holiday.

Dr. Chan called Friday and again on Saturday with updates regarding Robert's status. Robert's lithium levels had dropped to normal range, but now he had a sodium imbalance and was not responding to treatment to lower it. He was still semi-comatose and was a total-care patient (needing assistance in all activities of daily living). He was being nourished intravenously. I told Dr. Chan I would be visiting on Sunday and was looking forward to meeting him. He said he would arrange for me to meet on Sunday with the entire team involved with Robert's care.

Charline and I left early Sunday morning. The sun was shining, and the air was crisp. The roads were clean, and precipitation was not in the forecast. It had been several months since I had been out of our small town, and it felt good to see the countryside. We arrived at the hospital about midmorning and found Robert's room. He was in a room across from the nursing station, with no roommate.

When I saw Robert, he was lying flat on his back in bed with his wrists in soft restraints. He was covered to the waist with a sheet, and a catheter was draining urine. He was not aware that we had entered the room, nor did he respond to our greetings. He was agitated and repeatedly attempted to move his hands to pull on his catheter. When I bent over and kissed him, his skin had a stinging, salty taste. His moustache and eyebrows were coated with a thin, white film of salt. His body seemed quite warm, but I couldn't tell if he had a fever.

I went across to the nursing station and inquired about Dr. Chan. They said they would page him. A few minutes later, he, a resident, and the unit's attending physician came to the room. They said Robert wasn't responding to treatment to lower the sodium levels and had developed a slight fever. He wasn't able to eat or drink fluids on his own. They felt that if his condition remained unchanged, they would discharge him to home on hospice care on Tuesday morning. I asked them how long he would probably have left. Dr. Chan responded, "Two days to two weeks."

I felt numb. The hope that had lit my Christmas candle had been extinguished. There were forms to complete and papers to sign. I went through the motions on autopilot.

Charline and I left the VA at about midafternoon to begin the drive home. I was so thankful that she had made the trip with me, that I hadn't had to drive that distance by myself. We were trying to accept the doctor's words, but both of us were in a state of shock. We stopped on the way home for a lunch/dinner and were home about seven. It had been a long day.

THE ROLLER-COASTER RIDE

I SLEPT LATE THE NEXT morning. I was still numb when I awoke. Knowing I would lose Robert someday was one thing. Knowing that it might be later in that week was overwhelming. I couldn't grasp it.

I decided I would call the kids and let them know what was happening. It was the legal holiday, so they wouldn't be working. I normally would have called and wished them "Happy New Year."

I told them I was going to see Robert at the hospital on Sunday and that they should be expecting my call with an update. Talking with each of them was very therapeutic for me. Their caring thoughts and concern were warm fuzzies, and I was in need of all the warm fuzzies I could get. I assured them I would be okay and keep them posted regarding changes in Robert's status. His children had each said their good-byes at their last visit and wanted to remember their dad as the vital and energetic person they had always known.

Robert and I had discussed what we would do when one of us passed away while we were living in New Mexico. All our family members were so far away. To have all of them make the trip to New Mexico seemed ridiculous. We had decided that the surviving spouse would take his or her mate's ashes to Florida and have a celebration of life at a funeral home in Gainesville. It was centrally located, so friends, students, and family could all gather with a minimum of travel time and expense.

We had told them of our idea, and they all thought it was a good one. My daughters asked if I needed help or company. I told them I felt I could manage and I would rather have them save their leave time for when I came to Florida.

Once I finished my phone calls, which took hours, I decided to check Robert's room and make sure everything was set up for his care and comfort. He'd be home the next day, probably by noon, and I wanted to be prepared for his arrival. I felt I might need more pull-ups and decided to go to the store to get them. As I was getting ready to leave, Charline called to see how I was doing. We decided to go out for dinner that evening. I had forgotten all about eating, and it sounded like a good idea to me. She picked me up, and we went shopping and then found a restaurant that was open on the holiday. We had a long, relaxing dinner.

When we got back to my house, she came in with me to chat for a while longer. There was a message on my answering machine. It was Dr. Chan asking me to return his call as soon as possible. My first thought was *Robert's gone. He'd passed away while I was out having dinner.* It was not supposed to be that way. It was supposed to happen at home, not in the hospital. I was supposed to be with him. He was not supposed to be alone. I hadn't said good-bye or I love you or anything. No, it wasn't supposed to happen that way.

I placed the call and waited. To reach a doctor, my call had to go through the switchboard, be transferred to the unit, and then to the doctor's extension. It seemed to take forever. Finally, Dr. Chan answered. He told me that Robert had finally started to respond to the medication they had been giving him to bring down the sodium levels. They had come down significantly in the last twenty-four hours. Robert was more alert and was responding to his surroundings. If his status continued to progress positively for the next eight to ten hours, they wouldn't be discharging him in the morning. He would remain an in-patient until his condition was completely stable. Dr. Chan said he would call with an update on Robert's status in the morning.

I think I thanked Dr. Chan before I hung up. I don't remember. I hope I did.

Charline could tell that something had changed. When I told her what the doctor had said, we hugged and laughed. Then I cried, and we hugged some more. It was a miracle. I could hardly believe it, but I wanted to believe it. I *would* believe it.

Suddenly it seemed as if a heavy weight was lifted from my heart. Robert would come home, not to die, but to be with me for who knew how long. Years maybe.

I got two glasses from the china cabinet and filled them with wine. Charline and I toasted to "health and happiness in the New Year." Yes, Happy New Year, everyone!

MIRACLES—ALIVE AND WELL

THE NEXT MORNING, THE RINGING of the phone again awakened me. I jumped out of bed and went to the kitchen to answer it. I was sure it would be Dr. Chan with a report on changes in Robert's condition. I was surprised when instead it was Gerald, our contractor. He hadn't been working on the house over the holidays because he was waiting for our new windows to be delivered. He said they had been back-ordered, and he was expecting them to be available the next day. Once the windows arrived, he would put them in the newly extended house front and then knock down our present living-room outer wall.

I updated Gerald on Robert's situation and told him I was hopeful Robert would continue to make progress and be kept in the hospital until he was stable. I told him that if the news wasn't positive, they would be transporting him to the house, and I would want the inside of the house to be kept intact for the time being. The remodeling project would have to be put on hold. I said I would contact him later that day, as soon as I heard from the doctor.

Gerald said he understood and would wait until I called before making any further plans. When I hung up, I looked at the clock. It was nine. The doctor probably wouldn't call until eleven; that was his usual time. I wanted to call him immediately, but instead I made some coffee and got dressed. My thoughts were in overdrive. I had forgotten all about the remodeling project; I had been so focused on Robert and his changing health status. Inside the house, the changes already made to the exterior of the house were not apparent. In my recent state of mind, that translated to "out of sight, out of mind."

When the phone finally rang, I was almost afraid to answer. If the news were bad, Robert would probably already be en route. But I thought Dr. Chan's voice sounded upbeat. I asked if Robert had had a good night. He said, "Why don't we let him tell you himself."

Then I heard Robert say in a weak but clear voice, "Lee? Are you there?"

I could hardly believe my ears. I had thought I might never hear Robert's voice again—ever—and there I was, actually talking to him, *and* he was alert and coherent. I don't remember most of what we said, but he did want to know when I could come and see him. I told him it would be soon, in a couple of days; it would depend on what the doctor had to say.

When I talked with the doctor, he said Robert had continued to progress positively through the night, and his lab values were good. However, he couldn't predict what

Robert's end level of function would be. They would begin with eating and toileting, and see how much independent activity he was capable of. Also, they would assist him in regaining his strength and mobility. It would probably be nearly two weeks before Robert would be ready to be transferred from the hospital to a nursing home, where he would need more rehab. He also said Robert was allowed to have visitors.

I told Dr. Chan I would plan to visit Robert toward the end of the week. I asked him to tell Robert that I would call him that evening so we could talk again.

After I hung up the phone, I just sat very still for a few minutes. I was numb again. It was hard to take it all in. But at least now it was because of good news. I felt like I should pinch myself to be sure I wasn't dreaming or hallucinating. I finally got myself a cup of coffee and thought about the last few days—and then about the next few days. My thoughts were again in overdrive.

Finally I called Gerald. I told him the new game plan for Robert and said we could proceed with finishing the living room. I also asked him what I needed to do to prepare the room. He said all the furniture would need to be pushed to the far inside wall and covered with drop cloths to protect it from dust and dirt. Also, I would need to remove all the fragile items from the tables, walls, and fireplace area. I told him I would get the room as ready as I could and that tomorrow would be fine to start the last phase of the remodeling project we had begun back in September.

Next I started calling people to pass on the good news. First I called Charline. Then I started with the kids. They were all at work, but I felt this change in plans merited interrupting whatever they were doing. With the two-hour time difference, it was midafternoon in Florida, and I felt I would be able to reach everyone. It is *so* much easier to share good news, and it was very uplifting for me to deliver my message—a message much different from the one just two days before.

When I talked with Stephen, Robert's eldest son, he said that after I had called on Sunday saying Robert would be on hospice, he had made arrangements to fly out to see his dad. He was hoping he might get there before Robert's final hours. He would be arriving on Saturday, the seventh of January, and stay for a week, leaving the following Sunday to go back to work.

I was so surprised and happy he was coming. When I told Stephen of the change in his Dad's condition, he was also surprised—and happy. Now, instead of a wake, Stephen could actually see and talk with his dad. I suggested we go to the hospital on Sunday, the day after he arrived. We would make further plans then.

That evening I told Robert I had a surprise for him. I would be coming to visit on Sunday, and I would bring someone with me—Stephen. Robert was very pleased to hear that. He sounded so well—and so normal. He didn't remember my visit on New Year's Day or anything about the last ten days. I told him we had all been very worried, but it seemed that things had turned around, and he was going to be much better now.

It felt *so* good to be able to talk to him again and to actually communicate with him. I told him how much I missed him and loved him and that I was looking forward to seeing him in a couple of days. He sounded a bit spacey and unsure of himself, but I was hopeful that it was just part of his recent trauma.

Being able to hear his voice was a blessing to me. I knew I now would be able to wait patiently to see the total extent of his recovery. When I considered the progress that had occurred in just the last three days, I knew that miracles do indeed happen.

EVERYTHING IN FLUX

ROBERT CONTINUED TO MAKE PROGRESS during the rest of the week. Each day there were new victories on his path to increased health and independence; he was eating well, toileting with assistance, going to physical and speech therapy, and communicating spontaneously and coherently. I was so happy to have my Robert back.

Gerald was putting up support beams and knocking down the support wall. The weather was cold, and even with the windows installed, the living room was very cool because the attic area was exposed. Gerald hung a tarp to help keep the cold out, but it wasn't very effective. It took layers of clothing to stay comfortable.

I was kept busy preparing for Stephen's visit, making sure I had food and other supplies in the house, talking with Robert, getting updates on his status from the doctor, and making plans with the hospital staff. They wanted me to meet with the social worker when I came to visit. That meant staying overnight on Sunday to attend the conference Monday morning. I called some friends who went to the VA frequently and often stayed overnight. I inquired about hotels in the area close to the hospital and made the necessary reservations.

The days flew by, and Saturday seemed to come quickly. Stephen arrived in the late afternoon. I hadn't seen him for over three years, and it was comforting to have him there with me. I felt like I wasn't so alone in dealing with the incredibly difficult situations that seemed to present themselves constantly.

We left for the VA Sunday morning. I had made arrangements for Charline to come over that evening and also the next morning to feed Lady and give her a little loving. We planned to be back early Monday evening, and Gerald would be there working Monday, so Lady would have some company during our time away.

Stephen and I arrived at the hospital before noon. Robert looked very good—well, comparatively speaking. He had lost a great deal of weight, his face was drawn and gaunt, and he was wheelchair-bound, but he could respond appropriately, hold a conversation, and even had a sense of humor. We were all very happy to be together, and our visit was like a celebration. Stephen and I stayed until midafternoon and then left to check into the hotel, which was several miles away. We returned again around suppertime and left about eight so Robert could go to sleep.

We returned the next morning, and I met with the social work staff to discuss discharge planning. They felt it would be about a week before Robert would be ready to be transferred to a rehab facility. However, we needed to begin that process right away to make sure there was a bed available when it was time for his transfer.

I needed to decide on a facility and make the initial arrangements. It really wasn't that difficult a decision; there were only two in our small town. Several years earlier, I had taught the LPN academic nursing program and supervised my students during their clinicals in both of the facilities. My first choice was the New Mexico State Veterans Home. It was an excellent facility with qualified and caring staff. The population was all veterans, mostly men, and I felt Robert would have a great deal of camaraderie with the other residents. He had been a cadre/drill instructor in the army and could swap stories with the other vets. I asked him where he would like to go for his rehab, and he also thought the Veterans Home would be a good place.

We left Robert about midafternoon for the two- to three-hour return trip home. Since the discharge date was uncertain, we planned to return to the hospital on the following Saturday so Stephen could see his father before leaving for Florida early Sunday morning. The return trip was uneventful and relaxing. We stopped for dinner about mid-journey and arrived home in time to feed Lady, who was very happy to see us.

During the next few days, I was in a sort of dream state. Sometimes I felt like I was a queen. Cooking was one of Stephen's hobbies especially breakfast meals. So I was served omelets or pancakes or French toast every morning—and all I had to do was show up. I also felt like I had a genie in a bottle when Stephen volunteered to sort out and organize the varied assortment of tools and junk that had accumulated for the last several years in the work and storage areas of the garage.

My genie also switched the furniture in the two bedrooms, making the front room next to the remodeled bathroom into a second bedroom. This was what I had wanted to do for Robert earlier, before he had become incapacitated. Stephen had managed a furniture store at one time and was experienced at moving large, bulky pieces of furniture. Good thing! This job included moving a piano, a large desk, five tall bookcases, a large chest of drawers, and a double bed.

The move wasn't far, but the doorways and hall were narrow, and the spaces were small and difficult to navigate. We worked together as a team and got the whole job completed in one evening. It had been such a long time since I'd had someone to help with things around the house. My genie seemed heaven-sent, and I do believe he was.

Gerald was making progress with the living room, but the constant pounding was very disturbing and annoying. On Wednesday, Stephen and I decided to escape from the noise. We drove to one of Robert's and my favorite spots: an area in the nearby mountains. Southern New Mexico is mostly desert, and the majority of vegetation is limited to small, low-to-the-ground plants and varieties of cactus. However, in the upper elevations you'll find lush forests of pine trees and mountain streams. The air there is clean and fresh, and since it was January, it would be crisp. If the sun were shining brightly, it would be warm, even though the temperature was near freezing.

We drove on the winding but well-paved road around the mountain until we reached an area where the trees form a canopy overhead and a little stream trickles down through a small valley area. This was the spot, and it was beautiful and quiet and peaceful.

There were no other people in the area, so it was a place of respite. Just being there made me feel good. It was a place to recharge my batteries, to refocus and renew. However, Stephen wasn't as comfortable with the heights and sheer drop-offs. He had lived most of his life in Florida, where the terrain is flat and the altitude is at or below sea level. For some people, the adjustment to these differences can be difficult and anxiety producing. For me, just being in that area was a sheer delight.

Thursday we visited a nearby state park that houses New Mexico's largest lake. It's formed from a dammed portion of the Rio Grande River and is a large recreation area for the state. The lake area is a pleasant change from the arid desert surrounding it.

We spent the following day canvassing our small local stores for gifts and mementoes from the Southwest for him to take back to Florida. The culture here is quite different from the Southeast, and it's quite a novelty for tourists visiting for the first time. In the evenings, Stephen and I played cards— something Robert and I had enjoyed doing with Stephen and his wife when we all lived in Gainesville, Florida.

As the end of the week approached, the time of Robert's transfer to the Veterans Home was confirmed: Sunday morning. I contacted the Home for an appointment to do the admission paper work, and we met with the admissions coordinator late Friday afternoon. Completing the paperwork was a lengthy process involving detailed financial and personal information and Robert's medical history. When we finished, I gave Stephen a tour of the facility so he would have a mental image of where his dad would be staying during his rehab period.

Our trip to the hospital on Saturday was pleasant with little traffic. Robert looked much better, and his level of function had improved. He was excited about his discharge and the transfer to a place closer to home. He and Stephen enjoyed their visit and said their good-byes.

Stephen told his dad that he and Lynette were planning to visit again during the summer. She had never been to the Southwest, and they would visit Arizona and the Grand Canyon prior to seeing us. Robert liked that idea. It was easier to see Stephen leave knowing Robert could look forward to their next visit only a few months away.

It seemed like Sunday morning came very early, and Stephen left to catch his plane for Florida. It had been a whirlwind visit packed with so many events and differing experiences. I was sad to see him go. I was so grateful for his company and all his help and assistance. It was sheer pleasure for me to have someone so capable and energetic to just be there with me when everything was in a state of flux.

FYI Commentary

How do you choose a nursing care facility?

Choosing a nursing care facility may seem mind boggling initially. However, the list of choices for final consideration should be determined by the same criteria used for choosing any place of residence: (1) Does it meet my needs? (2) Is it affordable? (3) Is the location acceptable? Some compromise among these factors is often necessary to make the final decision.

1. Patient needs

Your primary care physician is usually the person who confirms the need for a nursing care facility. His or her recommendation will be based on the diagnosis, prognosis, and care options. Does the patient need long-term or short-term care, rehabilitation or maintenance care, specialty care or generalized medical and nursing care? Your physician will determine the type of facility needed and the level of care required and make a list of appropriate care facilities to consider.

2. Affordability

This is often the major determining factor in making the final choice among viable options. What resources are available to pay for patient care: private insurance, personal financial resources, Medicare, Medicaid? Is the patient being directly transferred from a hospital stay for follow-up care? Does the facility accept Medicare and/or Medicaid payment?

3. Location

If there are multiple facilities to choose from, location may further influence your choice. Is the commuting distance for family members reasonable and manageable? Is the facility in a desirable neighborhood that's safe and comfortable for visitors? Is adequate parking available close to the facility?

Once you've narrowed the list of facilities to those that meet the above criteria, the final choice will depend on the quality of care provided and the patient's personal preferences. The order of the following list may not be consistent with your priorities, but hopefully the items listed will provide food for thought to include in your decision-making process.

- Is the facility clean, odor-free, attractively appointed, and comfortable? Does it "feel good" when you're there?
- Does the facility have a good reputation? Check with friends, other residents, or family members of residents. You might also find reviews and other information on the Internet.
- Is the staff friendly to and respectful of the residents and visitors? Do they work efficiently and appear competent? Is staff visible and busy, or just sitting around or out of sight?
- Is the food service area (dining room) pleasant and clean? Is the food nutritious and tasty? Does it meet the patient's needs?
- Are there visible safety precautions available and in use? Are there outdoor enclosed areas with patient access? Is there an intercom system or facility

communication system in use? Are camera monitors in use at exit areas? Are wander alerts being used? Are assistive devices available and in use?

- Are a variety of social events and group activities provided daily to promote resident socialization and stimulation?

Take your time, and check out these items. Visit unannounced on both weekdays and weekends. Visit at different times of the day: morning, afternoon, evening, and at mealtimes. Eat in the dining room. Is the food hot and attractively served? Are patients with eating problems receiving appropriate assistance? During the day, are most patients out of bed, dressed appropriately, odor-free, and well groomed? Are they out of their rooms and in an area that promotes socialization? Are call lights answered in a timely fashion?

Your personal observations of these conditions within the facility will help to reassure you that the care provided is *quality* care.

For his first admission to the Veterans Home, Robert needed short-term rehabilitation, or restorative care. He was being transferred directly from a hospital stay and needed skilled follow-up care. This qualified him for Medicare and private insurance payment for up to ninety days. There was no additional out-of-pocket expense for his care. Since my locality had only two choices available and I had prior professional experience with both facilities, my choice was quick and easy to make.

ALMOST HOME

STEPHEN'S PLANE DEPARTURE TIME WAS at six thirty in the morning, so he left for the airport at three o'clock in the morning; it was a two-hour drive to the airport and a one-hour preflight check-in time. Robert was not arriving until about ten thirty, so I decided to go back to bed for a while.

It was a short but restful sleep, and I was at the Veterans Home at about ten fifteen. I guess I was anxious to get Robert settled in and closer to home. The paperwork was already done, so it was just a matter of waiting for the ambulance.

The facility was pleasant to be in. It had formerly been a children's hospital. There were floor-to-ceiling windows in the common areas that made everything bright and sunny and cheerful. It was attractively decorated, and the sitting areas were comfortable and inviting.

I read the Sunday comics and part of the paper. When I finally looked at my watch, it was nearly eleven o'clock. I decided to check with the admissions coordinator to see if she knew why they were delayed. While we were talking, her phone rang. It was the ambulance driver. They had gotten lost and were calling for directions. They had driven past the exit off the interstate and were about forty miles south of the facility.

They arrived just before noon. Robert was very happy to finally reach his destination. He said he had to direct the driver again regarding the right exit to take to the Veterans Home. They were going to drive to the next exit north, which would have been an additional six miles out of the way.

Robert was in a two-person room near the nurses station. He didn't have many personal belongings with him, so getting settled was quick. They brought his Sunday dinner on a tray to the room. We were both excited and happy; it was so comforting to have him in the neighborhood.

Later the doctor came in to examine him and fill out the admission and physical exam paperwork. Robert seemed to be doing well—just a little weak. He would start physical therapy the next day and hopefully be able to ambulate on his own before discharge.

After the doctor left, Robert and I went exploring. I pushed him in his wheelchair, and together we toured the facility. I wanted Robert to be aware of the many options for interacting with his fellow residents. There were various areas to sit and visit or read. One hall was called Library Hall, where many residents were sitting, playing cards or games. It had tall bookcases filled with books and games— all available to the residents. We went to the canteen area, where anyone could buy snacks and a variety of other articles. There was also a craft room where residents worked at various long-term projects.

We had missed Sunday bingo in the auditorium, but we were assured that there were many opportunities to play bingo throughout the week—some in the afternoon and some in the evening. There were also movie nights with popcorn and drinks. We found the activities schedule for the month, and it seemed like residents could be busy all the time if they participated in the many activities available to them.

We went outside. The sun was still shining brightly. There was a large front porch on the facility with a view of the expansive green lawn surrounding the building. Walkways led to small gazebos placed strategically on the lawn. The grounds were well kept with tall trees for shade, and flowers and shrubs completed the landscaping. We could see the mountains in the distance, and parts of the town were visible. There also were two courtyard areas formed by the various wings of the building, and one had a beautiful sculptured fountain in the middle of it. The other had covered sitting areas with tables and chairs for enjoying the outdoor air and sunshine. The courtyards were also abundant with shrubs and trees and flowers to enhance the ambience.

I told Robert that I would like to live there if I could no longer take care of myself. I also said I hoped he would take advantage of the many activities available to him during his stay there. He didn't appear to be as positive about his surroundings as I was.

I stayed and had supper with him. We ate in the dining room with the other residents. The staff was friendly and helpful. Of the120-some residents, most of them ate their meals in the dining room. There were about six males to every female, and the residents ranged from mildly to severely impaired. The food was good, and the portions more than adequate. Robert seemed to enjoy his meal and ate well.

After eating, we went back to his room. It was January and already dark outside. We were both tired, and the staff was assisting residents with their bedtime routines. Robert and I talked for a bit. I told him I would bring him some clothes and personal items and be back in time for the noon meal the next day. His physical therapy would keep him busy for most of the morning.

I told him how happy I was to have him back home. He reminded me, "I'm not home yet—but—I will be soon." I hugged him, and we kissed goodnight.

As I walked to the car, I took a deep breath. The air was crisp, and the evening sky was dark. The lights of the town were visible from the parking lot. It was a beautiful night and Robert was home. Well, *almost* home.

A SHORT STAY

· ·

THE VETERANS HOME WAS LESS than three miles from our house. That made visiting very convenient, and I visited Robert nearly every day. I would eat the noon meal or the evening meal with him, and sometimes both. We would go to the various activities together. When there wasn't an activity he wanted to participate in, we would play cards or Scrabble or go to the canteen.

Robert started to play the piano for the other residents. He played by ear, and if he knew the words to a song, he could play it. He knew most of the oldies and goldies. The residents loved that and would call out requests. He didn't always get the melody right, but they didn't seem to mind or didn't realize it. He loved playing for them. It was an ego trip for him.

He worked hard on his rehab and attended physical therapy faithfully. He soon started using a wraparound walker most of the time, instead of the wheelchair. He was also taking care of his grooming and toileting and showering with less and less assistance. He was eating well and had gained back some weight.

As he started to regain his strength and his ability to care for himself, he began to get anxious about going home. He began to notice that many of the male residents were bitter and angry and negative, and he didn't want to identify with them. Their negativity had an influence on him, and he became increasingly dissatisfied with his situation. That was another reason I tried to spend as much time as I could with him.

Meanwhile, the remodeling of the living room was progressing, and Gerald projected it would be done in early February. I had bought a new curved sectional sofa and new coffee tables for the room from a store in Las Cruces. They were originally to be delivered right before Christmas. However, when Robert's health failed and the remodeling project was modified to include the bathroom, the timetable changed.

I had called and told the furniture store about our change of circumstances, and they were holding the furniture for us until further notice. I had picked out new carpeting, and it had been ordered and would take several weeks to be delivered. The men who laid the carpet were from out of town and only came to work in the TorC (Truth or Consequences) area on Saturdays.

We were replacing the carpeting in living room, hallway, and three bedrooms. This meant everything needed to be moved into another room and then back again after the new carpet was down. I really didn't want Robert to have to deal with all the chaos of that process. I also had to make trips to Las Cruces to buy new blinds for the living-room windows and several other items we needed.

Trying to work around the various schedules of the workers and companies involved was difficult. It became even more complicated once Robert decided that he didn't want to stay at the Veterans Home any longer. "I can get physical therapy from Lewis at home, like I did before," he said. "I don't belong here. I want to come home. I need to get out of here!"

I tried to explain to him the various aspects of my problem with his return to our unfinished house and asked him to be patient. But patience had never been one of Robert's stronger qualities. Once he had made up his mind about something, it was very hard to dissuade him from doing it.

The staff felt he should stay until the end of February; he would have completed six weeks of physical therapy, which they felt would be more beneficial for him. It was February 5, and he was threatening to walk out the door of the facility if they wouldn't discharge him. We haggled for several days, and finally I got him to agree to a compromise. The carpet-layers were coming the eleventh. I would need a day to put things back in place once they were done, so I proposed Monday, February 13. That would give the staff time to get his meds and paperwork ready, and I would have things more livable at the house when he returned. We finally agreed that I would pick him up late in the afternoon on February 13.

HOME AGAIN. BUT IS IT HOME?

ON FEBRUARY 13, WE PULLED into the driveway of our house. It was about four o'clock, and Robert was very excited about coming home. He was amazed when he saw the outside front of the house. He commented on the nice job Gerald had done. No one could tell there had been any alterations made: the house looked as though it had been designed that way.

Then we went inside, and Robert was overwhelmed. The living room seemed huge to him (it was over a third larger), and we had three times as many windows. The furniture had been rearranged to fill the added space. We still had the same furniture, but it looked very different on the new carpeting. The old carpet was multicolored shades of gray and had been in the house when we bought it. It was over fifteen years old, dark, and quite worn looking. The new carpet was oatmeal color and felt plush when walked on. It made the house look brighter and more spacious.

Each bedroom looked different, too. Well, the bedrooms *were* different. I had moved the study to the smaller, middle room across from the kitchen. It had been in the large, front corner room that was now the guest room. The old study had two floor-to-ceiling bookcases that were now in the garage because the new study was much smaller and couldn't accommodate them. The computer had been moved from an area in the kitchen into the new study. The whole house seemed to have changed since he had last seen it.

I must admit, I guess it had. We had both planned the addition, but when he became debilitated he wasn't that interested. Although he knew about the changes as they were being made, the finished product was impressively different. He had been gone from the house for nearly two months and was very sick for several weeks prior to that.

Although the changes had occurred slowly, he hadn't witnessed the transformation process. It was as though he was Rip Van Winkle; he had returned to find his world totally changed. He had come home, but home as he had known it was no longer there.

The change from a hospital or nursing home environment back home often is traumatic, but in this case the time warp was really overwhelming. I hadn't realized before this writing how strange the first days back from his long hiatus must have been for him. Home—that comfortable space we'd lived in for the last five years—was no longer home. Home had become a strange, new world.

REMARKABLE CHANGES

THE FIRST WEEKS OF ROBERT'S return were a continuous celebration of his improved physical strength and function. He was able to perform his morning activities independently: showering, dressing, shaving, and grooming. He could walk around the house without a walker or cane. He got his own breakfast and often his own lunch. I told him I would help him in whatever way I could, but he would have to ask; that way he wouldn't feel I was hovering over him like a mother hen.

Our follow-up appointment with Dr. Spruce was about a week after discharge, and she was elated to see his progress and increased function. We got the prescriptions refilled and the order for Lewis to begin physical therapy. Lewis started coming twice a week. Their goal was for Robert to be able to walk around the block without a walker or cane within the next six weeks. Each week Robert got stronger and was able to walk a little further.

The new living-room sofa and tables came, and we rearranged the furniture again—pretty much for the last time, because the curved sectional couch would fit in the room only one way. Robert had refused to use the lift chair since his return. "It's for sick people, and I don't need it" was his statement concerning it.

We decided to have a garage sale to get rid of the extra furniture and other items we no longer needed. However, I did keep the lift chair in the guest room, because I didn't know how long Robert's recovery status would last. Because Parkinson's is progressive and debilitating, I knew he would likely need the chair sometime down the road. Charline and I worked the garage sale, and Robert enjoyed meeting and talking with all the people who came and showing them his rose garden.

Robert and I went out to eat once again. We both enjoyed that. His appetite was good, and he liked seeing our old friends. I took him to McDonald's so he could see his Geezer Group, but he didn't feel comfortable with them anymore; he felt he didn't fit in. I think he was having some problems keeping pace with their conversation.

I had noticed some other changes in Robert's mental status and his behaviors. When I would mention past events, he would have little or no memory of them. He started going through our old files and paperwork: records from high school, college, work, etc. It seemed as though he was trying to fill a void in his memory, trying to trigger it through reviewing the documents. He started going through books that he had treasured for years.

Robert had a photographic memory when he was younger, so once he'd read a book or seen a movie, he could recall it in detail from memory. His books didn't seem to mean much to him now; it seemed he could no longer grasp their meaning. Though they were wonderful books of ancient history and civilizations with many full-page color pictures, and they were in mint condition, they seemed to have lost their appeal to him. We also had a set of encyclopedias that he had previously used for resource information. He decided he wanted to give them to the local library. We gave the history books to the library and the encyclopedias to a private children's school.

Robert also gave away some personal items that he had had for a long time. If someone commented on it admiringly, he would give it to that person, right then and there. With my background as a psych nurse, I began to wonder if he was depressed and possibly thinking suicidal thoughts.

I began to observe Robert's behavior more closely. He didn't seem to have any other obvious signs of depression, such as feelings of negative self-worth. One day when he was again going through old paperwork, he threw some items in the wastebasket. I asked him about them, and he said he was just thinning the files, adding, "There's no need to keep all this stuff." I looked through the papers and I had to agree with him; he hadn't thrown away anything of importance. However, from then on I checked the wastebaskets to make sure he wasn't discarding something I might want to keep.

One day I found his Social Security card and a current credit card in the wastebasket. I asked him about that, and he responded, "I just had too many cards in my billfold. I wanted to make it lighter. A billfold shouldn't be too heavy in your pocket." I took some important documents from the files—like his birth certificate, our marriage license, and his military discharge papers—and hid them in a dresser drawer to make sure they didn't come up missing when I needed them.

Other things that Robert was doing weren't normal behavior for him. He was trying to be independent. For example, he decided to help clean up the table after meals. He would gather up the dishes and utensils then turn on the cold water, put a dish in the stream, run his index finger over each dish, give it a shake and place the dirty, wet dish back in the cupboard with the other clean, dry dishes. He would do the same with the silverware, glassware, cups, and anything else that had been used for the meal.

I found this behavior very difficult to cope with. So when I was preparing a meal, I would wash and dry each item before using it. Every few days I would put all the items in the dishwasher and start again with a clean slate. He was like a two-year-old trying to help Mommy. I appreciated the thought, but he was causing me a lot more work.

I struggled with what to do. It seemed to make him feel good that he was able to help. Finally I decided to adopt a new mantra: "What difference does it really make?" I would look at the situation, and if the answer were none, I would repeat my mantra. I often had to say it over and over when I had to deal with his not-so-helpful behaviors.

He also tried to help me with the housework. One day I was washing windows in the bedrooms and bathrooms, and he decided he would clean the screens. He found a stiff wire brush and proceeded to scrape the lower half of the screens to remove the dust that our New Mexico winds had deposited there. The brush created large holes in the screens. The mosquitoes found easy entry into the house in the evening and at night, and I was one of their prime targets. This behavior did make a difference, so I asked him not to clean any more screens for me.

I finally realized how much Robert's judgment was impaired; his decisions weren't rational. I had read earlier that one of the effects of the prolonged toxicity and resulting chemical changes in body chemistry often was permanent brain damage that led to a form of dementia. I felt this might explain the changes in his mental status: his impaired judgment, his memory problems, and his lack of insight into his own behavior.

I also was beginning to question if he really had Parkinson's disease. There were no tremors; he could again walk without assistance; he could perform his self-care independently. How were these behaviors consistent with Parkinson's—a chronic, progressively debilitating disorder?

Robert had been on neuroleptic medications for over twenty years. On occasion, he had been on mega doses of these drugs, which have Parkinson's-like side effects. I wondered if they were the cause of his symptoms that led to the diagnosis of Parkinson's. I decided I wanted an evaluation by a physician specializing in Parkinson's disorder.

I had attended a seminar on Parkinson's about a year or so earlier. The main speaker was a neurosurgeon who was performing deep-brain stimulation procedures in Albuquerque. She had done procedures on two of the members in our Parkinson's support group with very positive results. She not only preformed the procedure, she also screened all the candidates to confirm their diagnosis prior to the surgery. Robert knew about the procedure; one of the recipients was a friend of his at the Veterans Home. I asked Robert if he would want to have an appointment with her for an evaluation. He said yes.

I called the doctor and made an appointment with her. We wouldn't be able to see her until the end of April, which was nearly two months away. I was hopeful she could answer my many questions.

QUESTIONS BUT NO ANSWERS

IT WAS MARCH AND TIME to focus on the rose garden. The pruning had been done in the fall, but now there was weeding, digging water wells, mulching, and getting things ready for the new growth of spring. Robert wasn't able to walk in the yard easily, so I appointed him supervisor. He directed from the patio and was the resource person when questions arose. It worked well—he liked his role, and I found gardening very therapeutic. It was physically tiring for me and kept Robert occupied and out of trouble.

Robert's attention span was short for most things. He couldn't sit through an hour-long TV program. He preferred music and liked to hear his CDs and old records. He tried to do crossword puzzles as he had in the past, but he rarely completed it in one sitting; he would lose interest. Usually he would go back to it later and finish it.

We spent most evenings sitting on the patio, watching the sun go down and the stars come out. It was calming and pleasant for both of us. Sometimes I would start our table fountain and/or light a candle to add to the ambience. I tried to take Robert out for a ride or trip each day—to the grocery store, the park, Dairy Queen, McDonald's, out to eat, etc.— just to keep him busy and occupied.

The time seemed to pass quickly, and I soon turned my attention to our upcoming trip to the doctor in Albuquerque. I had never driven through that city and wasn't familiar with it. I had gotten good directions from the doctor's office and had a city map. I routed the trip on the map and tried to get a mental picture of the route fixed in my mind.

My experience with driving in big-city traffic was very limited, and my poor eyesight made such a trip very intimidating. I couldn't read road signs until I was very close, almost passing them. I asked Robert, who'd had 20/20 vision, to be my spotter, and he agreed that he would. He was able to read a sign almost before I could even see it.

On April 28, we set out for his doctor's appointment in the big city. It's over 150 miles to Albuquerque on an interstate, and the driving is easy until you get to the city itself. When we got there, I asked Robert to watch for my landmarks. He tried, but as we were passing the first one, I realized he couldn't focus long enough to be of any assistance to me. I tried to recall the route, and I actually found my way without a problem, although my anxiety level was very high.

The doctor's appointment went as scheduled. She asked Robert for his medical history. When he was unable to answer her questions, he referred her to me, saying, "She knows me better than I do."

She gathered information regarding both his past medical and psychiatric history. I told her my concerns regarding the original diagnosis of Parkinson's disorder, his episode with the toxicity, the coma, and his current recovery status. She gave him a physical and a mental status exam, plus a neurological exam. She had him walk and listened to his speech, trying to get as complete a picture of his functioning as possible. As she was doing the exams, she was also typing the results into her computer. When we left her office, we left with a printout of the workup she had done.

Her findings were inconclusive; she couldn't say if Robert had Parkinson's or not. His recent "recovery" would indicate he might have originally been misdiagnosed. However, the toxicity-induced coma may have caused a temporary reactivation of the part of the brain responsible for Parkinson's disorder—a deep-brain stimulation that would wear off with time. This could explain his recent "recovery."

On the other hand, the symptoms that led to his original Parkinson's diagnosis may have been the result of long-term neuroleptic use. There was no way of making a diagnosis at that time. She suggested we taper his Parkinson's medications and finally stop them, then wait and see if the Parkinson's signs and symptoms recurred. Also, she suggested we consult a psychiatrist to adjust his psychiatric medications.

So we made the trip back home. Our questions had not been answered; they had multiplied instead. One of the leading doctors in the field couldn't tell us what we were dealing with.

MORE REMARKABLE CHANGES

WHEN I USE THE WORD *remarkable*, it's in the clinical sense. When used in medical documents, it means "the observation of something uncommon, unusual, or abnormal." Much of Robert's behavior was now remarkable. It wasn't normal for the man I had lived with for over twenty years. We had always been able to talk things over, to discuss issues logically and with reason.

Two days after we returned from the appointment with the neurosurgeon, Robert announced that he was no longer going to take his medications—any of them. What he had gleaned from the doctor's report was that no one knew exactly what was wrong with him, but he had gotten well on his own. He believed that the doctor said he didn't need to take medications anymore.

I tried to reason with him. I told him that the doctor had said to stop the Parkinson's medications—not the diabetes and psych meds. Diabetes and bipolar disorder were confirmed diagnoses, and they needed to be managed to ensure his quality of life. The consequences of no management would be predictably negative. He wouldn't listen to me; I had no credibility. All my nursing experience told me this was not a good idea, and it was so unlike Robert to think that it was. I panicked.

I called Dr. Spruce and told her my story. She reminded me that a patient has the right to refuse treatment. No one could force Robert to take his medications. She suggested that I bring him into her office for an appointment. She would see if she could influence him to reconsider his decision. I asked Robert if he would talk with Dr. Spruce. (Really, I *pleaded* with him.) He finally agreed, and our appointment was for the next day. The meeting was less than fruitful. Our attempts to cajole Robert fell on deaf ears. He was adamant regarding his right to refuse his medications. No arguments we made would dissuade him.

As a health care provider, I had always been a fervent patient advocate. Too often patient rights were compromised or suppressed in the name of expediency or financial concerns. I always encouraged patients to exert their rights and assisted them with information and support in doing so. I thought, *Well, maybe Robert will do fine without all those medications.* Certainly he had managed his diabetes before with diet and exercise. Maybe that was possible again. Regarding the bipolar disorder, I thought maybe Robert's body chemistry had changed with age. It has been documented that older persons with a history of mental illness sometimes mellow, with their symptoms lessening or even going away. Maybe he would be fine with no meds. Maybe.

Well, I wasn't able to wear my health care provider hat for very long. Instead, I became the informed wife and caretaker who was living with a man whose behaviors might prove disastrous to him and to me. As a psych nurse, I had repeatedly witnessed the consequences of patients not taking their medications. It was not a good scenario, and the only thing that seemed to resolve the situation was for the patient to resume his medications. The life of a spouse with an unmedicated bipolar partner usually was a living hell.

My previous coping mechanism—my "What difference does it really make?" mantra—just wouldn't work for me anymore. It *did* make a difference—a huge difference! I became angry with Robert and his decision. I had managed to cope with the two-year-old behaviors my spouse had exhibited, but I just didn't see how I could cope with an independent adult male whose thinking and judgment were impaired and who would eventually become delusional and psychotic.

A HOLDING PATTERN

AFTER THE INITIAL SHOCK OF Robert's announcement and my futile attempts to change his mind, our life settled back into its previous routine. In retrospect, I would say I settled into a comfortable state of denial—big-time denial! I couldn't change his decision, yet I knew the results would probably be negative. So I just accepted the present and tried to live as though things wouldn't change significantly.

The month of May in New Mexico could be described as magical. The brown desert areas and bare trees and shrubs seem to come alive. Our garden plants, and especially our roses, respond to the longer, warmer days and burst forth into bloom—all at the same time. The trees were leafed out, and everything was green and vital. Our back yard was a spectacular array of color. There were between forty and fifty rose bushes, and sometimes as many as a dozen flowers bloomed on one bush alone. We had multiple shades of red, white, orange, yellow, pink, and lavender blossoms.

The roses are usually at their best in early May. Each bush will have a couple of blooms throughout the summer, but only one or two bushes bloom at a time. In the heat of the summer, they aren't so productive, but in September or October, they have another flush of growth and new life. It's not as grand as in the spring but it, too, is beautiful. I'm very responsive to the beauty of nature, and when I allow it to permeate my awareness, it's very therapeutic for me. Enjoying the magic of our rose garden helped to balance the chaotic nature of my domestic life.

I had become a working psych nurse again due to Robert's behaviors, with one significant difference: I didn't have the validity and clout that an inpatient psych nurse has. I had worked in a veteran's hospital most of my career. In the military, nurses are officers and are treated with the respect and authority of that rank. However, I had none of that with Robert. He was making his own decisions and wouldn't listen to input from me.

Nurses often make insider jokes or comments with each other about their profession to relieve stress and help them get through their shift. One comment often heard is "Once a nurse, always a nurse." The nursing mind-set isn't left behind when the scrubs come off. Your nursing behaviors accompany you home, to the mall, to the grocery store— wherever you go. If you see a stranger struggling with a physical problem, you probably step in.

Psych nurses are trained observers of subtle behaviors and mannerisms. They practice their skills wherever they are. I couldn't forget my background. I knew Robert's mental status would gradually change over the next month or so. During that time, there would be enough residual medication in his system to help him maintain some control of his thoughts and his anxiety level. In the second month, the deterioration would be more pronounced until he reached baseline. This information allowed me to relax for the time being.

June came, and Stephen and Lynette arrived in time for Father's Day. They stayed for a week. It was a very pleasant break from our usual routine, and that was good for Robert and for me. They had been made aware of his noncompliance with his medications and of our resulting domestic stress before they arrived.

Robert was demanding but otherwise able to interact without incident. Stephen wanted to keep busy and asked what he might do to help. I had two requests: (1) get our red car cleaned and ready to put up for sale, and (2) entertain or keep an eye on Robert so Lynette and I could have a girls' day out in Las Cruces. He agreed to both requests.

Robert and I had two cars: a red town car and a gray highway car. We usually traveled together around town and drove the red car. When we made a longer trip, we used the newer, bigger, and heavier gray car. If we took separate trips, Robert drove the red car, and I took the gray one. Robert had given up driving a year ago and there no longer seemed to be a need for us to have two cars. We had discussed this before his hospitalization and had decided to sell the red car. However, because of the pace at which everything happened during the latter part of that year, we hadn't managed to take care of the matter. New tags and insurance were due in July and it seemed like a good time to try to sell the extra car.

Stephen showed Lynette the town and the lake area. They spent part of each day out of the house, experiencing the local color. We played cards several evenings; Robert tried to play the first night but only lasted one hand. I think he couldn't concentrate well enough to play for a longer time. He chose to listen to music instead.

Lynette and I chose Thursday for our girls' day out. We would take the gray car to Las Cruces and do some shopping, go to a movie, and have dinner. Stephen decided to use that day to wash, wax, and detail the red car. We said we would be home before dark, which was around eight thirty. The men could go out for dinner wherever they chose.

We left about midmorning on Thursday. It was such a treat to have a day away from the house—and from Robert. I hadn't been out of town since our Albuquerque trip. I knew Robert and Stephen were together, so I could really relax and feel carefree. We shopped. We enjoyed a movie. We had a very nice, relaxing dinner. It was a lovely day. I didn't even have to drive; I just directed Lynette where we needed to go. By the time we got home, Stephen had finished the car. It looked almost brand-new, ready for the "For Sale" sign. What a great day it had been!

Stephen and Lynette left early Saturday morning to fly back to Florida. It had been a very pleasant visit. The house seemed so quiet once they were gone, and I had a feeling they probably would not make another trip to the Southwest.

I put the "For Sale" sign in the car window. The next week, a FedEx driver who was delivering a package asked about the car. I gave him the information, and he said he would call me. The next day Gerald, our contractor, and his family came by to show Robert their twin babies. He also asked about the car. Then he called his in-laws on his cell phone and relayed the information. They came over immediately to look at it. After a few questions, they decided to buy it. The next day we exchanged the title and car for cash, and our red car was gone.

That evening the FedEx driver called regarding the car. He has wanted it for his daughter to drive to college classes from their rural home near Las Cruces, so he was very disappointed when I told him it had been sold.

We were now a one-car family. This left more garage space, and Robert started to spend more time sitting in the garage. We had a patio table and chairs stored there, and Robert would sit out there with the garage door open and watch the neighbors and the cars go by. It was an area protected from the heat of the sun, and he could see the mail woman deliver the mail and the children across the street playing in their yard. It all seemed to have a calming effect on him.

It was the end of June and almost two months since Robert had stopped taking his medications. I didn't feel comfortable leaving him alone for any length of time, so I would invite him to accompany me to run errands. I had expected his mental status to be noticeably impaired by then, but he seemed pretty much intact. We appeared to be in a holding pattern. I thought maybe he was right. Maybe he *was* healed.

THE BUBBLE BURSTS

··

DURING THE FOLLOWING MONTHS OF July and August, the bubble of denial that I had been hiding in burst. Robert became increasingly agitated and less cooperative. His eating habits changed; he started eating excessive amounts of sherbet (which is loaded with sugar) and ice cream (one of his favorite foods). He started getting up earlier in the morning and spending more time in the garage and by himself. His grooming habits had changed, too; he showered less often and shaved infrequently.

He also became obsessed with the idea of moving to Florida. He felt his life would be better in Florida than it was in New Mexico. In psychological terms, this is called seeking a geographical cure. I tried to reason with him. I pointed out that Florida was the same now as when we had left. The humidity, mosquitoes, traffic congestion, and hectic pace of life compared to New Mexico were still there. The kids were still busy working and living their lives and wouldn't be any more available than they had been when we lived there. Many of our best friends had moved away. Also, he wouldn't have his garden to enjoy.

I suggested we go to Florida for a visit. The problem was how to get there. Robert wouldn't fly, and I told him I couldn't drive there. I had never driven that kind of distance in my life, and I didn't feel comfortable doing it now. I suggested the train as an option. He refused to ride the train. I wasn't unhappy that he refused; I didn't relish several days on a train with him in his condition. So we were at an impasse.

His judgment was becoming more impaired. He started to leave all the doors of the garage open—front and back— as well as the door into the house. Lady would go into the garage with him, but once he turned his attention from her, she would run away, and he wouldn't be aware that she was gone. There is a leash law in TorC; if she were reported and picked up, they would take her to the pound.

The first time she was gone, I found her in the yard next door. I asked Robert to please make sure Lady was in the house and that the house door was shut whenever he went into the garage. However, he didn't remember. The next time she was nowhere in sight—and I was very upset because she didn't have her tags on. They had fallen off in the yard several times, and I had kept them in the house so she wouldn't lose them. I called the radio station and the police department to report a missing dog.

We were just getting into the car to canvas the neighborhood when my neighbor drove by and stopped. He had seen her a couple of blocks away in someone's yard. We drove over there and picked her up. I guess I expressed my distress enough that Robert remembered to shut the door to the house from then on.

I would sometimes take Robert to the park. It had green grass, trees, picnic tables, and a view of the Rio Grande River. It was a pleasant place to spend time, and I thought it would be therapeutic for both of us. Robert would usually say hello as we passed people sitting in the park and often made a brief remark about the weather.

One particular afternoon, he saw two men sitting at a picnic table, and he started a conversation with them. It was apparent to me—because I had worked on a drug rehab unit for several years—that they were addicts and transients. It became apparent that they were in the park waiting while their female friend was buying drugs. We both watched as one of the men gave her money and she ran across the park to make the purchase. However, Robert was oblivious to all of this. He invited them over to our house to listen to his CDs, told them where we lived, and gave them our phone number and information about our lifestyle. I finally convinced Robert that it was time to go. That was the last time I took him to the park.

I decided to begin a thousand-piece jigsaw puzzle. I was hoping Robert and I could work on it together, because we could start and stop at will, and the puzzle would wait, unchanged, until we came back to it. It would be a very flexible activity that would result in something beautiful.

When we started, he was enthusiastic. However, he soon lost interest; he couldn't readily find any pieces that fit together, and he couldn't focus for very long. I continued to work on the puzzle and finally completed it about a week later. It was very relaxing for me. I could be present and observant, but it also allowed my mind to focus temporarily on something other than Robert.

TV seemed to agitate Robert, and he couldn't follow a story line for long. He didn't want the TV or the radio on. I tried playing some of our favorite videos and DVDs, but he would watch about a third of a film and then lose interest.

Robert tried to work the crossword puzzle in the paper but had difficulty making much progress. He would put the answers in the wrong blanks and then they didn't fit with the clues in the other direction. Often he just couldn't figure out what the answer was even to the easy clues.

I usually took him with me when I went grocery shopping. He had enjoyed grocery shopping and I thought he might like picking out items and making food choices. One day as we were checking out he said he needed to go to the bathroom. I said I would meet him near the store entrance when I was done checking out. When I arrived, he was talking to an elderly woman. He was asking her all kinds of questions, and she was obviously frightened by his manner. Because he was a big man he could look quite intimidating at times. She relaxed a bit after I appeared. I explained I was his wife and apologized if his behavior had alarmed her. I also intimated that he wasn't well. From then on, Robert chose to wait in the car while I went into the store for groceries.

It was Labor Day weekend and we had stopped at the grocery store. It had been raining and the temperature was cool so I left the windows of the car open for the fresh air. I wasn't gone more than ten minutes. When I returned, someone was sitting in the driver's seat. This stranger had been passing by the car, and Robert had started talking to him. The man told Robert about his sick daughter at home and how he had not been able to work the last week because he was a single parent and had to take care of her. Now his rent was due, and he didn't have the money. Robert had told him to get into the car and wait for me to come out of the store; that he didn't have any money, but I did, and I would give him some.

The man was probably in his thirties and had walked to the store. He was carrying a twelve-pack of beer and smelled of alcohol, though it was about nine in the morning. I opened the door to let him out of the driver's seat. I was quite sure any money he was given would go for drugs and alcohol and I didn't believe a word of his story regarding a sick daughter.

However, I did want him to leave so I gave him the only bill I had in my purse—a twenty—and wished him well. Robert then proceeded to offer him a ride home. He got into the back seat and directed me to his place. He lived in a rundown trailer park about three blocks from the store.

Robert also seemed to be preoccupied with our financial status; he would repeatedly call the bank to check on our account balances. I would find slips of paper on the desk on which he had computed our net assets. One day he announced that he had contacted an appraisal firm to determine the value of our house. They came and made the appraisal and said we would receive the report by mid-September. He was still pursuing the idea of moving back to Florida. I didn't want to move anywhere and certainly not under the current circumstances. I told him I would not move to Florida.

Robert's behavior was very unnerving and I was become increasingly vigilant. The only thing predictable about his behavior was that it would be inappropriate. Once he was convinced that I wouldn't move and wouldn't drive him to

Florida, he decided he would do it alone. He announced he wanted his set of car keys. I stalled and said I didn't know where they were. "Then I want to borrow yours," he said. What should I do? He had a valid driver's license, and he owned a car. I finally produced his set of keys, and the next morning when I got up, he and the dog were gone. It was about eight o'clock. I hadn't heard him get up or leave the house.

He finally drove into the driveway about nine. I was so glad to see him—and the dog—in one piece. I asked him where he had gone; he had just driven around town and through some other neighborhoods and then home.

We had planned to go to the senior center meal site for their hot noon meal that day. As we started to leave the house, he said he wanted to drive. I decided I needed to see what his driving was like, so I rode with him. He drove dangerously slow the less-than-a-mile trip to the center, starting to brake for the corner in the middle of the block. He also would forget to put on his turn signals. If he saw something of interest, he would just stop in the middle of the road to observe it. When we were leaving the center he insisted on driving back. Once we were home I told him I didn't think he should be driving; he wasn't safe behind the wheel. I also told him I wouldn't ride with him again.

He continued his morning rides. He would often leave at six—once it got light. I suspect he left that early because there would be fewer cars on the road. Often he would stop for breakfast downtown. Sometimes he would meet a friend there. Other times he and the dog would just go for a ride. One morning he left (I don't know how early), and when I got up, I found all the doors to the garage and the house wide open.

I felt so vulnerable and so helpless. He was out of control; his behavior was inappropriate. He wouldn't listen to a word I said. He was a menace on the road and driving *our* car. What if he had an accident and hurt himself, or hurt or killed someone else, destroyed property, injured the dog, or totaled the car? Since the car was jointly owned, I would be equally liable. He was a threat to our savings, our home, everything we had worked for.

Yes, the bubble had burst, and reality was crashing down around me.

TIME TO ACT

. . . .

I KNEW I HAD TO do something to resolve this situation before disaster struck, so I called the Motor Vehicle Division. I told them my husband was impaired and not safe to drive a vehicle. They told me that I would need to get a medical doctor's statement that he wasn't competent to drive and send it to the state MVD office. They would investigate and cancel his driver's license if warranted. Well, he wouldn't see a doctor, so that was not a viable option.

Friends suggested I disable the car. But then I would be without a car, and that wasn't a wise idea. Also, he would just call the garage and have the car fixed. Robert's judgment was impaired, but that didn't make him stupid. Others said I should take away his keys and hide them. But what about my keys? He would take them and have them duplicated. So these weren't viable options.

I called my friend Caroline, whom I had worked with at the Behavioral Health Clinic. I talked with her about doing an intervention with Robert and wondered if the psychologist who ran the alcohol and drug rehab groups might lead it. An intervention is a group of friends and/or relatives of an individual who come together in a supportive way to describe the behaviors of that individual and its negative impact on the people most important in his or her life. The group is usually about four or five key people who gather in an "impromptu" meeting with the person and confront him or her. The purpose of the intervention is to make the person aware of his or her destructive behaviors and motivate that person to seek treatment for change.

My friend presented the psychologist with my request. He pointed out that interventions are appropriate tools only for a person who can respond to reasonable thoughts in a logical way. Robert didn't fit that criterion, so that was another nonviable option.

Caroline did volunteer to come over to the house with her husband and try to encourage Robert to seek treatment. I jumped at the suggestion, and we set up the meeting. The couple had been friends of ours for a few years, and I knew Robert would welcome their visit. We all tried to reason with Robert in a gentle but very truthful, pointed way. It was to no avail. He refused to see a doctor or seek any kind of treatment; he insisted he was healed, so there was no need for him to see a doctor or take medication.

I decided to consult a lawyer for advice. One thing I was considering was a divorce so I wouldn't be financially liable for Robert's actions. The lawyer advised me that I probably couldn't divorce him if there was a question of his competency, even if Robert would agree to a divorce. He didn't recommend initiating that action at that time.

Robert's physical and mental status continued to decline. He wasn't able to sleep well, waking at four or five in the morning. He usually would go out and get the newspaper, which came between three and four o'clock. He could no longer bend over and pick up something without support; his balance and his gait were quite impaired. When he went out to pick up the paper, he would use the push broom to steady his gait and also to push the paper over to the car. Then he would lean on the car and pick up the paper.

My neighbor across the street told me that he had observed Robert fall in the garage while retrieving the paper one morning. He was about to come over to assist him, but Robert was able to get up on his own and didn't appear to be injured. The frequency of his falls increased, but thankfully without injury.

He was also becoming more argumentative and aggressive. He would go through his address book and call people he had not contacted for a long time. At first his conversations were not too out of the ordinary. However, over time, his speech became more garbled, and he made less sense; often his language would become rude or abusive, and frequently he would abruptly hang up. I witnessed this behavior toward several old friends of his. I called them back and explained, very briefly, some of his problems and apologized to them. I assured them he wasn't himself and asked them to forgive his inappropriate behavior.

Friends and other people in town were also telling me about his strange behavior. They would see him in a restaurant or observe him driving the car and call to see if I knew he was out there by himself. I told them I was aware but there was nothing I could do about it.

All this stress was taking a toll on me. I developed a painful stiff neck that didn't respond to heat packs or ointments. Finally, I went to see Dr. Spruce. I updated her on my situation and Robert's status, both physically and mentally. She gave me a prescription for a muscle relaxant, and I had a follow-up appointment in one week. I did get some relief from the pills, but my stiff neck was now chronic; it just wasn't quite as painful as before. My stress was constant, and pills weren't going to change that.

I went for my follow-up appointment, and she renewed my prescription. She also told me about the services of Adult Protective Services (APS). She said that since Robert's behavior was now mentally abusive to me, I needed to get a state agency involved in our situation; I needed to let the system intervene and protect him and me from the consequences of his irrational behavior. She gave me the phone number for APS and urged me to call.

My friend Caroline had continued to stay in contact with me and provide support. She had a client who recently had been in a situation similar to mine with her sister. Her client, LaVonne, was a social worker and had given Caroline permission to give me her phone number. I could call her if I wanted; they felt her story might help me to deal with my situation better.

I called LaVonne, and we talked. Her sister had mental problems, and her behavior became out of control. She wouldn't seek treatment or see a doctor. LaVonne was her sister's legal guardian, and she had to involve APS to get the situation resolved and to keep her sister safe. Talking with LaVonne helped me to realize that calling APS was the only viable option for me.

FYI Commentary

What is the role Adult Protective Services?

Adult Protective Services is a state agency that helps elderly adults (sixty-five years and older) and dependent adults (eighteen to sixty-four) who are disabled and unable to meet their own needs or are victims of abuse, neglect, or exploitation. The agency is responsible for investigating reports of abuse, neglect, and exploitation—usually within three working days. Referral can be made by a doctor or other health care provider, a neighbor, a friend, a spouse or other family member, or any concerned person who has observed one or more of these conditions. The agency investigates and provides or arranges for services to alleviate or prevent further maltreatment. These services include access to a social caseworker, case management, arranging for psychiatric and health evaluation, home care, day care, health care, and other social work services.

These agencies operate in each state in slightly different governmental frameworks. In many states, it's county-based, with each county having it own agency that's accountable to departments at the state level. In some states, the Department of Human Resources partners with the county agencies. In New Mexico, APS functions under the state's Aging and Long-Term Services Department and has only three agencies statewide. Contact can be made through a hotline number that can be found in a telephone book or online.

Why was it appropriate and necessary to get APS involved in my situation with Robert?

An adult is always presumed competent unless there is proof otherwise. An adult has the right to exercise free choice in making decisions. Only when an individual is deemed to be a threat to himself or others can this right be withheld, and then only when a court legally determines incompetency.

Robert was disabled both mentally and physically, with impairments that made him unable to take care of his own needs adequately and safely. By himself, he would eventually experience self-neglect. Because of his mental impairment with the accompanying poor judgment, his behaviors were intimidating to me, causing me emotional harm resulting in chronic pain, hives, chronic vigilance, and fear regarding my own safety. He was being emotionally abusive to me.

However, as long as I remained in our home and took care of his physical needs, there was no neglect occurring. His right to decide not to take his medications, see a doctor, or operate a vehicle were upheld. Adult Protective Services has the authority to investigate and act where abuse and self-neglect are suspected. I had to leave and allow his self-neglect and incompetency to surface before any legal action could be initiated. This would enable him to receive the help he so needed.

A DIFFICULT CHOICE

THE NEXT DAY I HAD another appointment with Dr. Spruce. I told her about my conversation with LaVonne the night before and that I had decided I should call APS. She said she would also contact them and talk to the caseworker about my situation. Then she told me that I would need to leave the house—to leave Robert to care for himself. She said I was enabling him to continue his disastrous behaviors.

Once I left, he wouldn't be able to take care of himself for long. Then, and only then, could APS intervene and have the authority to send him to the hospital for treatment, with or without his consent. This was the way the system worked. If I wanted their help, I needed to leave Robert to fend for himself.

She also assessed my physical and mental status. My blood pressure and pulse were the highest they'd ever been in my life; I wasn't sleeping well at night, so I was very tired all the time; my appetite was poor; my stiff neck was still painful; and I was very anxious. She told me if I didn't get out of my domestic situation soon, she would probably have to hospitalize me before Robert got treatment. She said I needed to start taking care of *me* and let the system take care of Robert. This wasn't what I wanted to hear, but I knew it was what I needed to hear and what needed to be done.

The next day I called APS. The closest office was in Las Cruces, and the caseworker came to the TorC area only on Tuesdays and Thursdays. It was Friday. I made an appointment for the following Tuesday afternoon, October 3, five days away. She said she would come to the house and interview both of us.

I also called my lawyer and made an appointment for Friday, October 6. I needed to update him on our situation and ask for advice regarding my leaving the house and Robert.

The APS caseworker, Maria, and her assistant visited the house midafternoon on Tuesday. Robert was home, and I hadn't mentioned anything to him about their visit. He was cordial and listened while they interviewed me. Then they asked if he would answer some questions. He agreed, but after some initial questions, he started asking them about the purpose of their visit and who had sent them. They told him Dr. Spruce had asked them to come by and see how he was doing.

Robert accepted that, but as the interview progressed and the questions became more specific regarding medical information, he became more guarded and started to turn the interview process around. He began interviewing Maria. When her answers were evasive or puzzling to him, he ended the interview, saying he was finished talking with her and suggesting she leave. She told him she would check back with him again on Thursday and gave him her business card.

When they left, Robert began quizzing me regarding their visit. Who were they? Why had they come? Who had sent them? What did they want? I played dumb, saying I had no idea but I felt it was thoughtful of Dr. Spruce to have someone come to check on him. Robert looked at the business card carefully and then put it on the table in a prominent place. I knew he wasn't satisfied with the explanations provided. I asked him if he would like to go to Dairy Queen for an ice cream cone, trying to divert his attention from their visit.

I was gone to the grocery store on Thursday when Maria came to the house. Robert went to the door but refused to let her in. She could see from their brief encounter that he was appropriately dressed and groomed, alert and oriented; that information was sufficient for her to complete her report of her home visit.

When I got home, Robert told me Maria had been there and that he wasn't letting her into the house again. He said he didn't understand what she was doing or why she was doing it. The next day, I called at her Las Cruces office and talked with her. I told her I was planning to leave the house and Robert the following week on Thursday morning and wouldn't be there when she made her visit. I told her I would call her that Thursday afternoon regarding my whereabouts. I had talked with Charline, and we had planned that I would go to her house with the dog and stay until things were resolved.

On Friday afternoon, I went to see my lawyer. I told him what had transpired and that I was planning to leave Robert the next week. I told him I felt certain that when I was gone with the car Robert would attempt to buy a vehicle and that we had enough funds in our checking account at that time to pay for it with cash. The lawyer advised me to withdraw the funds from our account via a cashier's check made out to our trust and to hide the check where Robert wouldn't find it. He also suggested I go to the four local car dealers and make them aware of the situation and that Robert was not safe behind the wheel. I would request that they not sell Robert a car. We agreed to a follow-up appointment in two weeks.

It was late Friday afternoon when I left the lawyer's office. I decided I would see the car dealers and go to the bank on Monday. Then I would have the rest of the week to prepare for my departure from my home.

I knew my departure was necessary, but I didn't want to do it; I didn't want to leave Robert. I felt like I was abandoning him, running away. Phrases like "until death do us part" and "in sickness and in health" kept running through my mind. How could I leave him just when he really needed my help? Also, I didn't like all the subterfuge—being evasive and plotting behind his back. We had always been open and honest with each other.

However, my logical mind and clinical experience told me this was the only way to resolve the situation so Robert could get the help he needed. I talked with both stepsons that weekend, and they were very supportive. They felt their dad might hurt me in a state of anger or confusion. They wanted me to leave as soon as possible. My sister-in-law was also concerned for my safety and urged me to come and stay with her. Caroline, my counselor friend, had the same concern and urged that I go—the sooner, the better. My head said, "Go!" My heart said, "Don't leave him now; he needs you." Would I ever get my head and my heart on the same page?

Well, reluctantly, I agreed. I would leave my home and my husband on October 12. I would remain homeless until Robert agreed to seek treatment and was following his doctor's advice.

PLOTTING AND PLANNING

WHEN I AWOKE MONDAY MORNING, Robert had already left with the car. I called Charline, and she agreed to take me on my errands. We went to the bank and discovered it was Columbus Day, so it was closed.

We proceeded to the car dealers. There were only four dealers, including new and used cars, in our small town. I went to each dealership and talked to the owner or manager. I explained my situation and that Robert shouldn't be driving a vehicle. I told them my lawyer had suggested that I contact them and ask for their cooperation. All four agreed. I said I would mail them a letter the next day reviewing our conversation and thanking them for their assistance.

It was very difficult sharing the details of my personal life with complete strangers and relating the most confidential aspects of Robert's health history. I felt I was betraying his confidence and airing our dirty laundry for the entire world to see. That evening, I composed the letter on the computer and had them ready for the mail pickup the next day.

I was very tired by the end of the day; I felt drained. As I prepared for bed that night, I noticed my lips were swollen. Then I saw there were some red blotches on my arms. Upon further investigation, I realized my face and entire trunk were covered with red blotches and rash-like spots. There were also areas on my extremities, but the breakout there wasn't as extensive. I wasn't having any difficulty breathing—another a good sign. I tried to diagnose the problem: No, I hadn't eaten anything different in the last couple of days. No, I hadn't been exposed to anyone with a rash—not that I knew of. No, I hadn't worked in the yard or with any chemicals in the house.

Because the majority of the outbreak was on my trunk, I decided it was internal in origin. The only new drug I was taking was the pain medication for my neck. I'd been taking it for weeks, and there hadn't been a problem. But I knew I might be having an allergic reaction to something, so I took a Benadryl and didn't take my pain medication that night.

I showed Robert my blotches and commented that I must be allergic to something. He said he could cure me because his hands had special healing powers. He said if he could lay his hands on my rash while we prayed together, my rash would disappear. I declined his treatment offer, but his words indicated how sick he was becoming and the urgency of my situation.

I was very anxious that night and had difficulty sleeping, despite being very tired. My head was spinning with thoughts of the day's events and the situation I was trying to deal with. Robert also wasn't able to sleep; he was up and down throughout the night.

In one of our conversations, he told me people were interested in buying or leasing our house, saying they wanted to film a movie in the neighborhood. He had told them he wanted to sell it and go back to Florida. I asked him when they had talked with him. He said it was that afternoon. I told him I would like to meet them and ask them some questions. He said he would tell them of my request the next time he saw them.

I now knew Robert's mental ability was becoming severely impaired: he was hallucinating, felt that he had special healing powers, and wasn't sleeping well. As his mental status declined, his thoughts became more irrational and bizarre, and his behaviors more and more inappropriate and increasingly harder to predict or control.

I finally did doze off to sleep early that morning for a short time. When I awakened, Robert had already left with the car. I called Charline and asked her to come over. When I opened the door to let her in, she just stared at me. I did look pretty grotesque. I had red blotches all over my skin, and my lips and eyes were very swollen.

I told her I wanted to go to the bank and withdraw the monies out of our savings and checking accounts and then check with Dr. Spruce about my outbreak to make sure I didn't have anything contagious. We left the house, and she drove to the bank. She waited in the car while I went inside. The bank people were cooperative, and I got the cashier's check. I left only about a hundred dollars in the checking account to cover outstanding checks.

When I returned to the car, Charline told me she had been thinking about my situation. She felt I shouldn't wait until Thursday to leave Robert; I should leave today—as soon as possible. She said she would help me; we could do it together. I felt I needed to check with Dr. Spruce before I made a decision, so we went to the clinic.

I explained my problem to the clerk at the window, and she called Dr. Spruce's nurse. The nurse said I would need to make an appointment, but it would be several days before the doctor could see me. I was trying to explain to the nurse that I only wanted to know if I had anything contagious or if it was an allergy to a prescribed medication. As we were discussing my problem, Dr. Spruce came into the office area, saw me, heard me talking/arguing with her nurse, and came to my rescue. She confirmed that it looked like an allergic reaction and I should stop the pain medication immediately. I also could substitute a common over-the-counter pain reliever if needed for the neck pain. I should continue the Benadryl for a couple of days until the rash and swelling were gone.

Charline and I left the clinic and returned to her car. I told her I agreed with her; I should leave as soon as possible. However, I didn't want to have a face-to-face confrontation with Robert about it. I couldn't predict how he would react, and I wanted to make my departure as uncomplicated as possible. I decided that when I was a safe distance away, I would call him on my cell phone. I would tell him that I had left him and would not return until he was seeing a doctor and following the treatment plan that was recommended. I would say that I couldn't continue to live with him unless he was physically and medically stable and under a doctor's care.

We sat in the car and tried to formulate a plan. I needed to go back to the house, get the dog and her food, collect some of my personal things, grab a few clothes, and take the car. I would also need to get Robert's set of car keys. Otherwise, if he were able to locate the car, he could take it. However, getting his keys might be difficult.

We were hoping he wouldn't be there when we got back to the house, but we made a backup plan to follow if he had already returned. We would have to collect the items and get them into Charline's car without him seeing what we were doing. We would alternate talking with Robert to hold his attention, so the other person could collect items and take them to the car. We would each try to pick up his set of keys whenever we could find an opportunity to do so.

Once I had my things in her car, Charline would say good-bye and drive away. She would then pull around the corner and wait for me. I would tell Robert that I was going to take Lady for a little ride, and the dog and I would leave in my car. I would pull around the corner and then follow Charline to her house.

As we left the clinic parking lot, I heaved a sigh of relief. We had just plotted and planned my escape.

ESCAPING

As WE WERE LEAVING THE clinic parking lot, I remembered that I needed to stop mail delivery to the house. I had no way of knowing how long I would be gone, and there would be bills coming. I needed to intercept them to make sure they were paid on time. We stopped at the post office, and I put a hold on the mail delivery; I would pick the mail up at the post office counter at the end of each week, until further notice. As I explained to the man behind the counter about my situation and asked how I should handle it, I started to choke up, and my eyes became teary. It was so hard to tell my story to strangers.

When I arrived at the house, Robert and the car were there. He was sitting at the dining-room table, eating orange sherbet from the carton. Charline and I greeted him, and I told him I had gone to the doctor to see about my rash and what Dr. Spruce had said.

"That will really make you sweet," Charline joked as Robert continued to eat the sherbet.

He promptly replied, "You can go to hell!"

We were both shocked. He normally wouldn't have spoken to a woman that way, and certainly not to Charline, whom he had joked with and teased for years. I knew we needed to execute our plan as quickly and as smoothly as possible. And I didn't want to confront him in his current mood.

I went about gathering my belongings and the items I needed for the dog. I just threw everything into a big beach bag and a couple of paper sacks so it would look like groceries. It was very hurried and haphazard. I mostly tried to make sure I had all my medications; anything else I could borrow from Charline or buy. Once I had my stuff gathered, Charline started taking it out to her car. I went to check on Robert. He was sitting at a table in the garage, reading the newspaper. He had placed his car keys on the table near the paper, and I couldn't pick them up without him seeing me.

Charline had finished loading her car and came to say good-bye. She hugged me and wished me luck. "See you around the corner," she whispered in my ear. She said good-bye to Robert and left in her car. I sat at the table with Robert for a couple of minutes and glanced at the newspaper briefly.

Then I went into the house and got Lady and her leash. I told Robert I was going to take her for a little ride. "I think she might like that," I said cheerfully. I want over to where Robert was sitting at the table. He was facing away from me, looking at something in the front yard. I came up behind him and kissed him gently on the back of his head as I reached for the car keys. He paid no attention to me. I quickly slipped the keys into my jacket pocket and got the dog and myself into the car in the driveway.

I felt like a combination of Judas Iscariot and Benedict Arnold, betraying Robert's trust, deceiving him, and now deserting him. He watched as I drove away with the dog. I waved as we left. It was about noon on Tuesday, October 10.

SEEKING SUPPORT

. . . .

I FOLLOWED CHARLINE TO HER house, which was about four miles away in a nearby town. We unloaded my stuff and let Lady explore her new surroundings. We made a makeshift bed for her with some old blankets so she would have an area that she knew was hers. Charline didn't have a fenced-in yard and I would need to walk Lady at least three times a day for her to relieve herself. I put on her leash and we went for a walk. The roads weren't paved and walking wasn't always easy, but the fresh air and exercise were a welcome break from the stressful morning I'd had. We were probably gone fifteen minutes.

While I was walking my thoughts raced. I felt guilty for leaving Robert to fend for himself when he was so compromised physically and mentally. I felt guilty sneaking away like a thief in the night. I decided to call the neighbors and alert them to the situation.

I talked with my neighbors on both sides and the three across the street. Again it was difficult to stay composed while explaining our situation. I asked them to watch the house for any unusual activity or problems (fire, strange noises, etc.) and to notify the police if they noticed anything strange. Dan and Jim said they would check on Robert periodically to see if he needed anything from the store. I knew that Maria from APS would check on him that afternoon. I also called the local police and asked them to drive by and check the house routinely. Everyone was very understanding and cooperative.

Not only were my thoughts racing, I also couldn't sit still. If I wasn't on the phone I was pacing. I guess I was frantically trying to control a situation that I had no control over. Robert called Charline at about three o'clock to ask if I was there and to tell me to come home. She denied I was there and told him she didn't know where I might be.

I called Maria to tell her that I'd left the house. I told her where I was staying and gave her Charline's phone number. She said when she stopped by the house Robert had answered the door but wouldn't let her into the house. He appeared unchanged from her previous visit.

I waited until about five o'clock to call Robert. I used my cell phone because we have caller ID at the house and he would recognize Charline's phone number. He wanted to know where I was. I told him I wouldn't tell him but that Lady and I were okay. I also said we wouldn't be coming back until he was under a doctor's care and following his plan of treatment. I added that I wouldn't live with him unless he was stable mentally and managing his diabetes. When he heard this, he said angrily, "You can go to hell!" and hung up.

It was so difficult to stay strong! I wanted to call him back and tell him I'd be right home and would cook him a nice supper. Instead, I called my counselor friend, Caroline, to update her regarding the changes that had occurred. We talked briefly and she said she would stay in touch. I fed Lady and Charline fixed us a sandwich for supper. I really wasn't hungry but I knew I should eat something. We watched a little TV and then I took Lady for a walk.

The night sky was clear, and the air was crisp and still. A sliver of moon shone brightly. I tried to find some calm within myself, to relax my tense body and overactive mind. I felt I had enlisted all available areas of support for Robert and for me. I knew I could no longer help him. It was out of my hands now. "Let go and let God." I had said that to patients so often on the drug addiction unit. I was learning it was easier said than done.

A STARK REALIZATION

· ·

CHARLINE AND I WATCHED THE news and then went to bed. It had been a very long and difficult day. I felt exhausted and was looking forward to a long, refreshing night's sleep. However, sleep wouldn't come. I kept processing the day's events, followed by scenarios from the past eight months— all the bizarre and irrational behaviors, the poor judgments, the flaring temper, the self-absorption, the total disregard for others and their feelings. All the episodes since Robert came out of the coma in January flashed through my mind— like troops marching for review in dress parade. I tossed. I turned. I tried to lie very still and relax my body with deep breathing, but my mind was merciless. It would not quiet. I got out of bed and went to the bathroom. I put on an extra blanket to be warmer. But when I went back to bed, the tape started playing again.

Toward morning, my thoughts about the situation seemed to change—to clear a bit and take on more focus. I began to realize that the man I had lived with for twenty-four years was gone. I had lost my best friend, soul mate, and companion in the foggy haze of December and January. The man that survived the coma was different, changed, someone I didn't know. I couldn't communicate with this person; he didn't seem to care about me or anyone else.

I realized that this person wasn't trustworthy. I couldn't depend on him to keep his word. Suppose he went to a doctor and started taking his medications again in an attempt to have me come back to him. Once things were running smoothly, what would prevent him from deciding not to take his medications or see a doctor, as he had in May? In the twenty-four years Robert and I had been together, he had always been faithful regarding his medication regimen. He knew that to manage his bipolar disorder, he needed to take his pills consistently and to consult his doctor if changes in his mental or physical status occurred. He also knew that to manage his diabetes, he needed to take his pills and watch his diet. He had never debated these facts in our twenty-four years together.

But the man who came out of the coma in January didn't recognize these facts. He had decided he no longer needed his pills; he thought he was healed. His thinking had been irrational then, and all the chaos of the last four to eight months was the result. What would prevent him from making that decision again?

I realized I could not trust this post-coma man to think rationally or to keep his word. I could not live with someone I couldn't trust. No amount of love would change his irrational thinking; no amount of patience could make him act responsibly. It would be like living with a time bomb—never knowing when it might go off. I realized that the outcome of this eight-month ordeal was that I could no longer live with Robert. I could no longer live with my husband!

MAKING PROGRESS

. . . .

WHEN DAYLIGHT CAME I DECIDED to get up, feeling drained and reeling. Yet I had a sense of relief. I felt that I had a direction, that I was no longer in the role of victim. I could establish some control of *myself* and get off the merry-go-round I'd been riding.

I had to feed and walk Lady, and at two I had an appointment with Robin, a counselor at a local mental health clinic. Dr. Spruce had recommended that I see her for support during this period of crisis. Today was our first meeting. These two activities would provide some structure for my day and help keep me focused. Charline said she would take me to my appointment. That way my car wouldn't be seen in town, and my whereabouts would be less apparent.

The session with Robin was intense. I told her of my realization of the night before, and she asked how I felt about it. I told her I didn't think Robert was capable of living by himself for an extended time and that he would need a caretaker for the majority of the day. Physically he wasn't able to perform household chores. His memory was impaired, and he would need help with his medications. He would need help managing his finances and paying bills. He wasn't competent to drive and would need help with transportation. I said I didn't feel he could live alone and he probably couldn't afford to pay for the amount of assistance he would need, even if he could find such a person willing to take the job. I felt he would need to be in a long-term facility.

Robin asked me again, "How do you *feel* about your realization?"

I had been telling her what I *thought* about it. I didn't know how I felt about it. I knew I no longer wanted to live with the post-coma man called Robert. The last eight months had been hell and I didn't want to risk a replay.

Also, I felt that I couldn't take care of him by myself physically. I related to Robin what the two of us had promised each other twenty-four years before, when we first realized we were in love. Both of us had had two previous divorces, and neither of us felt we were very good marriage material. We agreed that we'd stay together as long as it is good. What we meant was that as long as our love was mutually strong and we trusted each other completely, we would stay together. I told Robin I felt it was no longer good—our bond was broken.

I told her I would always love Robert and be there for him and help him in any way I could, but I would no longer live with him or be the victim of his irrational thinking and behaviors. I felt I owed it to myself to separate myself from the post-coma person who was now my husband. I felt

I needed to establish strong boundaries for my interactions with that man.

After my session, Charline and I went out for coffee at a restaurant near her house. I was feeling somewhat better. At least I felt calmer physically; I could sit quietly without the need to pace. My thoughts weren't racing, and the rash was barely noticeable. My eyes were still puffy, but my lips were normal. I didn't feel *good*, but I did feel *better* than yesterday—and better is always good.

Robert had called several times asking to speak to me while we were gone. We decided it might be a good idea if we moved my car. If it were visible, it would be obvious where I was staying and I did not want to risk a face-to-face interaction with Robert.

Charline called a friend who lived a short distance away but in a very private and secluded area. No one would spot my car there. Her friend consented. We took it to her house and left it there. Now I not only felt homeless but also without a vehicle.

That evening we watched TV. It had been a long time since I'd sat and watched TV for an evening; Robert hadn't wanted the television on, saying the voices and the music bothered him. It was very relaxing to watch the evening soaps, as I called them. I didn't know any of the characters or the story lines, so Charline had to fill me in. It was confusing but a nice distraction; I wasn't thinking about my situation.

Then Lady and I went for our evening tour of the neighborhood. The night was quiet and peaceful. I felt calmer. It would be some time before I could say I felt quiet and peaceful, but for then, *calmer* was good.

When Lady and I returned from our walk, we all retired to bed. I slept much better that night.

GETTING FEEDBACK

. . . .

THE THURSDAY-MORNING SKY WAS GRAY when I awoke. I didn't want to get out of bed, but I knew Lady was hungry and needed to go outside. The morning air was damp and cold and promised rain. We walked in the misty air for about half an hour before we returned to the house.

Charline was watching TV. She's an avid TV watcher and had the set on from early morning until bedtime. I usually listen to music during the day—whatever kind of music matches my mood or desired mood. It's generally light classical or easy instrumental with no vocal. I find that most relaxing and I can concentrate on other things without the music interfering. So the TV noise sort of bugged me. "I guess that's a sign I'm feeling better," I mused.

I picked up the paper and read some of it. Then I worked the puzzle page—all but the crossword puzzle. That was part of Charline's morning routine, and she had already completed it. I wasn't accustomed to spending time leisurely watching TV and working puzzles. For some time, the chaos had begun when I got out of bed in the morning and lasted all day. Walking the dog was often my only respite activity.

I tried to ooze myself into a half-dozing, half-awake state and just sit there and relax. I was not very successful, but it was a pleasant experience.

Late that afternoon my neighbor across the street called. Jim had gone over to see Robert and reported he seemed to be fine. Robert had asked him to pick up some milk, bologna, and ice cream for him the next time he went to the store. When he returned from the store, Jim had taken the groceries inside the house to see how things looked. Everything seemed to be tidy, except for some dirty dishes in the sink. I thanked Jim for helping out and for the update.

That afternoon Maria from APS called. She had visited the house and this time Robert asked her to get him a chocolate milkshake. When she returned with the shake he let her into the house. She said everything looked in order, and Robert was clean and dressed appropriately. He was pleasant and able to carry on a meaningful conversation. She said she would check again the following Tuesday and give me an update. I thanked her for the information and for helping Robert.

Things seemed to be calming down. Robert was maintaining. I was starting to relax, and Lady and I had established a routine that appeared to work for her. I was sleeping better and had regained some appetite. Charline was enjoying our companionship.

Late Friday morning my back-door neighbor, Lois, called. Lois and Marty were in town for the weekend with their granddaughter, Jackie. Jackie had selected Robert as a surrogate grandfather, and whenever they were in town, she would visit him. Marty was a retired circuit judge, and they lived in Mesa, Arizona. The house in TorC was a vacation home; they would periodically come there to go fishing, boating, etc.

When they arrived on Friday Jackie had gone over to visit Robert. When she went home she told her grandmother that Robert had said, "Lee doesn't live here anymore." He had also told Jackie that he was going to buy a car—a blue car.

So Lois and Marty went over to investigate. They talked with Robert and learned I had left on Tuesday. They noticed Maria's business card from APS on the table and a note pad with a list of names and phone numbers. One was for the local taxi service. Lois asked Robert where I had gone and he told her he didn't know, but probably to Charline's house. He gave her Charline's phone number. Lois called to ask if I felt it was safe for Jackie to visit him—and, of course, to hear what I had to say about the situation.

I told her I thought it would be fine for Jackie to visit; Robert would probably very much enjoy spending part of his day with her. I filled her in on the events of the last few weeks and my motivations for leaving when I did. I asked her to keep me posted if she noticed anything else of importance.

I wasn't surprised by Lois's news. I had predicted Robert would try to buy a car. But I felt confident that the car dealers wouldn't sell to him, and of course he had no funds in the bank to buy a car.

However, on Saturday morning Jim called and said there was a car in front of my house with plates on it from Turtleback Motors, a local dealership. A young man had gone into the house and then come out and assisted Robert into the car. Then they had driven away together. I thanked Jim for the info and immediately called the Ford dealership. I got someone in the parts department. He said there wasn't anyone else there right then because it was Saturday. He said a salesman, the owner's son, would probably be back in the office soon; he had been there but had left just a few minutes before. I told him my story and asked him to have the salesman call me when he returned. He said he would do that.

I didn't know what else to do. The manager's wife had been very pleasant and had agreed to cooperate when I had been at the dealership earlier that week. Maybe there was some confusion or miscommunication. Yet I had also sent the letter; surely they had received it after five days. Then I was comforted by the memory that there was no money available to buy a car anyway. I decided there was nothing I could do but wait. I waited until about three o'clock in the afternoon to I call Turtleback Motors. There was no answer.

On Sunday afternoon, Lois called to say they were leaving to go back to Arizona. When they had visited Robert that morning, they noticed a wine bottle on the dining-room table. He seemed to have been drinking Saturday night but he seemed to be doing all right. I thanked her for the news and wished them a safe trip home.

When I thought about her observations, I was surprised. Robert rarely drank alcohol because of his medications and his diabetes. Then I remembered: Robert wasn't the person he used to be. Post-coma Robert was "healed"; he had no problems and took no medications.

PLANS GONE AWRY

On Monday morning, I called Turtleback Motors. The manager's wife answered. I asked to speak to the manager, and she asked who was calling. I told her my name, and I could hear a change in her voice. When Mr. Manning answered, he sounded defensive. I reminded him who I was and reviewed my visit of a week earlier and his wife's promise that Turtleback Motors would cooperate. I also mentioned the follow-up letter I had sent. He denied receiving it. I told him I would hand-deliver a copy later that morning. He said that Turtleback Motors was in the business of selling cars and that if someone had a valid driver's license, could afford the financing, and wanted a car, they would sell one to him or her. He said they weren't in the business of health screening potential car buyers.

I replied that I hoped there would be no injury or loss of life or property because he had allowed an incompetent

149

driver behind the wheel of a car he had sold to him. He said he hoped so, too, and hung up.

Charline and I took a copy of my letter thanking them for their cooperation to the dealership later that morning. When I tried to give it to Mrs. Manning, she directed me to her husband's office, saying she didn't want to be involved. I introduced myself and handed him the letter, commenting that I was sorry he hadn't received the letter I had sent in the mail. It had been over a week; certainly that should have been enough time. He was guarded but tried to appear cordial. He took the letter, and we left the dealership.

On the way back to Charline's, we stopped at the post office to pick up the mail. The clerk checked and reported there was none. She said Mr. Hildebrandt had stopped the mail carrier, had canceled the hold, and had been getting the mail delivered for the last several days. She told me that there was no way they could legally refuse to deliver our mail to our residence if that was what he requested.

At two that afternoon, Jim called. He said there was a blue four-door Ford Taurus sitting in our driveway. Robert had just gotten out of the car and was walking to the house. He apparently had gotten an ice cream cone and had dropped it as he tried to get out of the car. He could hardly walk from the car to the house. I thanked Jim for the update.

I wanted to cry. Why was this happening? I felt I was in some kind of karmic chess game; no matter where I moved, it was always checkmate. I had tried to protect Robert from harm and have people there for him if he needed help; I had tried to protect our financial situation and get our bills paid; I had tried to keep him from behind the wheel to prevent an accident. I felt so victimized, so helpless. I felt no matter which way I turned, there was a roadblock—a dead-end. Why? I didn't deserve this. "Things happen in threes" is the saying. What would happen next?

My answer came the next day.

NUMBER THREE OF THREE

· ·

IT WAS TUESDAY. MARIA WOULD stop by the house and check on Robert in the afternoon. It was now a week since I had left him. It was also October 17—Robert's seventy-fifth birthday.

I've always loved birthdays. To me, a birthday is the only day of the year that's most special to the person involved. A few other people share your same birthday, but the number is small compared to the multitudes that celebrate the big national holidays. Often you may not even know someone who shares your day of birth.

I have always made a big deal of others' birthdays, trying to make sure they were celebrations with special food, decorations, presents, etc. The kids loved having birthdays because it usually meant a festive party. As you get older, some birthdays are landmarks—sixteen, twenty-one, forty. And when you're much older, the years that end in zero and five—like sixty-five, seventy, seventy-five—become very significant.

It was Robert's seventy-fifth birthday, and he was alone with no special notice being made—no party, no gifts, no cake, nothing. I felt bad for him. I wanted to call and say, "Happy birthday!" or bring him a cake with candles or—at least, something.

That was my heart talking. My head knew I would do none of the above. Nothing in our situation had changed, whether it was October 17 or any other day of the year. Today would be business as usual.

I walked Lady, read the paper, worked some puzzles, and watched TV. I had started a jigsaw puzzle on Sunday. The table was set up in another room. It was a pleasant break from the constant TV blare and gave me something different to concentrate on.

I was working on the puzzle when the phone rang. It was about two, and it was Maria. She related the following account of her afternoon visit that day: She had stopped by to check on Robert at the house. She found that he had fallen in the bathroom earlier in the day, having slipped on feces on the floor. He didn't appear to have been injured from the fall. He had also urinated in the bed. She had taken his blood sugar and found it was over four hundred. She called the ambulance, and they had taken him to the local hospital emergency room.

Maria said I should call there and talk to the staff. Robert hadn't taken his billfold with him, and they needed his insurance card and other information. She said her job description prohibited her from handling a client's financial papers or accompanying him to the hospital. She had cleaned up the bathroom, stripped the bed, and done Robert's personal laundry that had been soiled. She added that she would leave and lock the house behind her. I thanked her for all she had done and said good-bye.

I called the emergency room, explained who I was, and asked to speak to the doctor. I told him I was a retired psychiatric nurse and shared briefly what had transpired in the last ten days. He said Robert's blood sugar levels were in the seven hundreds, and he didn't know why he wasn't in a coma. Robert was extremely agitated, and they had him on an IV drip to lower his blood sugar.

The doctor asked what I wanted them to do with him once the sugar levels had come down. I said I wanted him transferred to the psychiatric ward at the VA hospital in Albuquerque. He reminded me they wouldn't accept Robert at the VA until he was medically stable, which might take a couple of days. I said to admit him to the local hospital for stabilization and then transfer him to the VA. I said I would come to the hospital ER within the hour with the documents needed to admit Robert to the hospital.

Charline drove me to my house. It was a strange experience to reenter my home under those circumstances. I checked all the rooms. Maria had left the bathroom spotless. The dryer was filled with Robert's personal laundry, and the wet sheets and mattress pad were on the floor of the utility room. The mattress on our king-size bed was still very wet. Everything else seemed to be intact.

Robert had spread the opened mail out on the coffee table. There were several bills there. Also, there was some paperwork from the credit union for the loan he had taken out to purchase the car. On the dining-room table was an empty bottle of homemade wine a friend had given us that spring. It had been in the refrigerator for months.

I also found the keys for Robert's new car and his billfold on the table. His insurance cards and his driver's license were there. I put his billfold in my pocket, and we left for the ER.

I gave the ER staff the information without seeing Robert or asking about his condition. I didn't leave his billfold or take him a change of clothes. Charline and I left and arrived back at her house around six o'clock—just in time to feed Lady.

It had been another eventful day, and I was tired. I walked Lady earlier than usual that evening, and our walk lasted a bit longer. As I processed the various events of the day, I realized there had been a change in my feelings as the day progressed. I had started out wanting to rescue Robert from feeling lonely and insignificant on his birthday. I felt sympathy and compassion for him in his aloneness. Later, when I was listening to Maria say she had sent him to the ER, I felt relief. Now he was safe. Now that the system was involved, they were in charge—not me. He would receive the treatment and assistance he needed. As I was admitting him to the hospital, I also felt a sense of freedom.

Once he was stable physically, the VA would treat his psychiatric problems, and then they would be able to evaluate his ability to live independently. *They* would be making the judgment calls; *they* were considered the experts and had legal clout. I had been but a lone cry in the night, and suddenly I felt the heavy burden of responsibility for Robert's safety and behavior lifted from me. It was now between Robert and the system. I was free.

As Lady and I walked, I noticed a bright half-moon shining. The air was clean and crisp. It was a beautiful night—a calm and peaceful night. I, too, felt a sense of calm and a new sense of peace, deep within my being.

STRANGE TERRITORY

. . . .

THE CALM OF THE NIGHT before disappeared in the bright Wednesday morning sun. My to-do list grew quickly. I called Dr. Spruce and related the events of the previous day and Robert's new circumstances. I asked if she would arrange for his transfer to the psychiatric ward at the Albuquerque VA hospital, request patient stabilization, and then get an evaluation regarding his competency to live independently, both physically and mentally.

I also asked her to request Dr. Cooper for an evaluation of Robert. He was the psychiatrist at the mental health clinic and worked in TorC part time to service its clients. I would eventually need two or three evaluations to establish incompetence. Dr. Spruce said she would see Robert on rounds later that day and initiate the transfer arrangements.

Next I called Caroline, my counselor friend. She worked with Dr. Cooper and could give him additional information regarding Robert's behaviors over the last eight months. I related what had happened the day before and my recent conversation with Dr. Spruce. Caroline said she would speak with Dr. Cooper.

I had an appointment with Robin at two that afternoon, but first I wanted to go by my house and collect the bills and paperwork there. So Charline and I decided it was time to take my car out of hiding. I needed to start taking care of business.

At the house, I did the laundry and checked the refrigerator for spoiled food. I also moved Robert's new car, which was in the middle of the driveway. This made room for my car and gave me access to the garage.

Robert's car was a Ford Taurus but a much newer model than our 1997 car. It was computerized and appeared very complex to me. I could find no information about it in the house or in the car. There was no bill of sale, no owner's manual—nothing but a set of keys. It had temporary plates in the back window. There was a copy of the loan agreement from the credit union, so I gathered up the bills and the loan document. I would stop by the credit union and ask how he had secured a loan.

I felt strange in my house. It was the feeling I'd experienced the day before when I first walked in after being gone slightly over a week. It was a sort of an eerie feeling, a weird feeling. I just didn't feel comfortable or at home, and I didn't know why. Maybe it was because of the circumstances of my leaving. Maybe it was because Robert wasn't there. Except for his coma hospitalization and rehab, he had never been away overnight unless we were gone together. We had lived in the house for seven years. Now he was gone, and

I knew he would never come back there to live. It had an emptiness that I had never felt before.

When I had finished the laundry, I put some more of my personal items in a bag, closed up the house, and left. I wasn't ready to stay there overnight. I needed the comfort and security of Charline's home; I needed her companionship and mothering for a while longer.

I shared my feelings about the house with Robin that afternoon. I told her it was almost as if there were a ghost or spirit there. It made me uncomfortable. As we talked, my feelings and thoughts became clearer. I had made the decision about a week before that I could no longer live with Robert. That was a decision based on logic. However, upon returning to our home I was beginning to experience the reality of that decision. We were separated and would never share our home and former lifestyle again.

QUESTIONS AND MORE QUESTIONS

MY APPOINTMENT WITH MY LAWYER, Mark, was timely; it was on Friday of that week, and I needed some advice. I had talked with the people at the credit union. Robert's car loan was approved on the basis of our excellent credit history and his monthly direct-deposit Civil Service annuity payments. They were over $2,000 a month. Therefore, even without funds in a checking or savings account, he was given the loan.

I had also called Turtleback Motors and inquired about the car registration and the other paperwork from the transaction. They said that since the car was in Robert's name only, they couldn't release that information to me.

These were issues I wanted to discuss with Mark—plus others. Should I divorce Robert to protect myself from his actions if he were allowed to live independently? What should I do about the car? Should I sue Turtleback Motors for the costs and fees incurred from the purchase of the car? What about our trust? Did I already have Robert's power of attorney for financial and health matters?

Once in Mark's office, I related all the events that had occurred since my last visit. Robert had been transferred to the VA the day before and probably would be hospitalized for three to four weeks, at least. My professional opinion was that he was incapacitated—physically incapable of caring for himself and mentally unable to exercise sound judgment in financial matters. However, my opinion wasn't relevant. What if he were discharged from the hospital to his own care? As his wife, I would be liable for his actions. Therefore, should I get a divorce to protect myself? Mark didn't know if I *could* get a divorce at that time, since Robert's mental status was in question. He thought we should table that issue for the time being.

He couldn't represent me in the matter of the car because of a conflict of interest: he represented Turtleback Motors as a business entity. He suggested I talk to Mr. Manning and ask if he would take the car back and cancel the transaction. I said I would do that.

Mark looked at our trust agreement. Robert had granted me his power of attorney for health care and financial matters without his being deemed incapacitated. However, Mark drew up papers activating the trust article, so I could present them when I needed to act in Robert's stead. They would also enable me to obtain the paperwork for the car and the license plates. And I would have the right to place Robert in a nursing home upon discharge from the VA.

Mark also initiated temporary guardianship papers. They would be effective within days; they had to first be approved by the court. This would allow me to take care of legal issues in a timely manner as Robert's representative. Once he had been evaluated, if he were deemed incapacitated, we would need to go to court for a hearing before a judge. Both parties would be represented legally, and Robert could accept or refuse to have me as his guardian. If he refused me, the court would appoint a guardian for him, probably a stranger to both of us.

When I left Mark's office, my head was reeling. We had covered a lot of issues in a short time. I felt better for hearing his advice, but I also realized the complexity of my situation. The road ahead was going to be difficult and the ride bumpy.

God grant me strength!

FYI Commentary

What do guardianship *and* conservatorship *mean?*

A guardianship is a legal right given to an individual, making him or her responsible for the food, housing, health care, and other necessities for an individual deemed unable to provide these items for him/her self. A conservatorship is the legal right given an individual to be responsible for the assets and finances of an individual deemed incapacitated.

The guardian is supposed to monitor the incapacitated person (the ward) to make sure the person lives in the most appropriate, least restrictive environment possible, with appropriate food, clothing, social opportunities, and medical care. The need for guardianship/conservatorship has to be established; the person has to be deemed incapacitated. Documents assessing the ability for responsible decision making for oneself and one's needs are presented during a court hearing. There are usually independent medical evaluations and reports presented.

Once incapacity is established and the scope of the ward's needs determined, a guardian and/or conservator is appointed. Usually candidates are the ward's family members or friends. The court routinely monitors the ward/guardian situation to ensure that the ward is being appropriately taken care of. These actions can be reversed if the ward's condition changes and he/she is no longer deemed incapacitated.

A MAZE OF PAPERWORK

IN THE MONTHS THAT FOLLOWED, my life became a maze of paperwork, phone calls, appointments, and shopping trips. It was filled with questions, doubts, and indecision. It was also filled with quick decisions based on hasty research and limited planning. My dining-room table became an executive-sized desk covered with files of information I needed to help me wade through the unknown waters of the legal system, the Medicaid system, the Veterans Affairs system, and the New Mexico Consumer Protection Division.

As I revisit those files now, I'm amazed at the volume of information they contain and the time and effort reflected by their very existence. I don't know how I got through that time; my guardian angel must have been helping me. It was certainly stressful—extremely stressful. It was strange new territory for me, and I felt unprepared for dealing with the issues. But I didn't have any other choice.

However, I did have the help of my lawyer, my Human Resources Services (HRS) caseworker, the VA social worker and doctors, and the Veterans Home staff. They provided guidance in securing the necessary forms and answered questions about how to fill them out. I also had my counselor, Robin, and Dr. Spruce to tend to my mental and physical needs, and Charline provided friendship, love, and support. I must not exclude Lady, who provided love and companionship unconditionally.

That said, it was still a horrendous ordeal. Added to the volumes of paperwork were the deadlines for their completion. The individual pieces of the puzzle depended on each other; the completion of one agency's paperwork was necessary for another player to fulfill its role.

I estimated Robert's hospital stay to be about four weeks. I would need to submit the medical application prior to his nursing home admission. I would also need to establish an income diversion trust to qualify Robert to receive Medicaid. I would need an activated power of attorney and legal guardianship to secure the needed documents and have them transferred from his name to mine in order to qualify him for Medicaid. To become his permanent legal guardian, I would need evaluations from three doctors, stating that Robert was incapacitated. These evaluations would need to come from the social worker and doctors at the VA in Albuquerque prior to his transfer to the Veterans Home in TorC. I would also need to spend down our life savings to qualify us for Medicaid. In addition to all these agenda items, I still had Robert's new car sitting in my driveway.

So I went to see Mr. Manning at Turtleback Motors the following Monday. I told him that my lawyer had suggested

I request that Turtleback Motors take the car back. Mr. Manning said he couldn't do that, but would allow me to sell the vehicle off their lot. I said I would think about that and be back later in the week to pick up the paperwork on the car and the license plate, if possible. By then I would have a copy of Robert's power of attorney.

I was very angry about the car. When I got home, I called the main office in Socorro and asked to speak to Charles Marshall, the owner of Turtleback Motors. I was told he was out of the country on vacation and should call back in two weeks when he returned.

I still hadn't driven the car. I went out in the driveway and looked it over carefully. It was a fine-looking car and had probably been a good buy. The interior looked like new, and it was equipped with many of the latest features; it was ten years newer than my car. So I considered keeping it and selling my old car.

I sat in the car and tried to visualize driving it. Logically, I wanted to like this car. However, it seemed I just couldn't. All I could feel was anger and frustration. I hated what it represented: all the frustration and anxieties of the last eight months, feelings of helplessness and futility, feelings of betrayal and victimization by people who had promised me their support, assistance, and loyalty. I knew I would never like driving that car, would never like owning it. It wasn't a matter of logic; it was a matter of the heart. I felt I needed to get rid of this car so I could get rid of my anger about how it came to be sitting in my driveway.

Several days later, when I received the document stating my power of attorney for Robert, I took it to Turtleback Motors. I secured the vehicle's paperwork and a second set of keys for it. The license plate hadn't come in yet, and they said they'd call me when it did. The next day I received a form letter and questionnaire asking me to rate my satisfaction with the service I had received from the dealer. The letter was from the main office in Socorro. I checked "not satisfied at all" and decided to wait until I received the license plate before I sent the letter back.

About two weeks later, the license plate arrived. Meanwhile, my anger about the whole car transaction wouldn't dissipate. I decided to write an account of my story, address it to Charles Marshall, and attach it to the comment section of the questionnaire. I mailed it on November 6. On November 8, I received a reply. It was from Danny, the owner's son. He reiterated the offer Mr. Manning had made to sell the vehicle for me. They wouldn't just take the vehicle back and refund the money for the fees, license, etc. Meanwhile, I had to make the first payment on the car loan and another would come due soon. This made me even angrier.

Friends and others who heard my story advised that I contact the Better Business Bureau and/or the Attorney General's Office. I decided to file a complaint with the Attorney General. I went online, got a claim application, and filled it out. I attached my account of how the situation had evolved. It was written in a narrative form with dates. I attempted to state only the facts, rather like a nursing note. It was a time-consuming endeavor, but actually was therapeutic for me to tell my story in an attempt to right what I felt was an injustice.

During that time, other items on my agenda needed attention. The papers for temporary guardianship were filed. We would file for permanent guardianship after Robert had been evaluated and only if he was deemed incapacitated. So I contacted Robert's doctor at the VA, who said they would need to wait until he had been on his medications for at least two weeks before they could evaluate his mental status. It might be even longer before they felt he had reached his baseline.

Of all the items on the agenda, my major concern was getting Robert qualified for Medicaid. I knew it would be a lengthy process; I had met with HRS regarding Robert when he was physically impaired the year before. However, I hadn't initiated any paperwork at that time. I'd called HRS for an appointment shortly after Robert's admission to the VA hospital. My caseworker, Marla, explained the procedures and the paperwork. I needed to file the completed application before Robert could be admitted to a nursing home, and it would take several months before he would be approved. We would have to pay out of pocket for his care until he was approved.

We also would have to spend nearly all our assets to meet the State of New Mexico's eligibility requirements. I would be able to keep the house and one vehicle as part of my spousal rights. I could have up to approximately $31,000 in assets— for example, cash, checking/savings accounts, CDs, stocks, bonds, notes, and life insurance. My gross monthly income could be supplemented from Robert's for up to a maximum of $1,650. The application itself was only five pages long, but collecting the information on income, resources, etc., and the multiple documents that verified that information for both Robert and me was very time-consuming and stressful.

Robert's gross monthly income couldn't exceed $1,869, but his income from his pension did exceed that. So it was necessary to draw up an income diversion trust agreement and establish a trust account to handle his monies. It needed to be in place shortly after he became eligible for Medicaid. Basically, this was an account in a bank where Robert's monthly pension monies were to be deposited. I was made trustee of the account, and it was my function to pay monthly disbursements from these monies, such as medical care costs, trustee fee, Robert's personal needs allowance, health insurance premiums, and any "community spousal monthly income allowance" that applied. Any monies that exceeded $1,869 were to be accumulated in the trust account. Upon Robert's death, the total monies in the account would go to HRS as reimbursement for the Medicaid payments made for his medical care while in the nursing home.

His approval by Medicaid was contingent on the completion of all these many agenda items, and I needed documented proof that they were all in place. Marla and I targeted January 31, 2007, as our deadline so Robert could qualify for Medicaid payments by February 1.

FYI Commentary

Where can you find information about Medicaid financial assistance for the long-term care of an elderly person?

There are multiple ways to find out about Medicaid assistance. Your doctor, friends, and family members might be sources for when you first feel that you might need to use this option. This can open the door for you to begin thinking and communicating with others about Medicaid. Also, your local senior center might have useful information.

However, some information may not be reliable. So when you're ready to get down to business, check online or in your local telephone book for an 800 number where you can get the phone number and location of the office nearest you. (For example, search for "Human Resources Division" or "Social Services Department.")

The Internet is an excellent resource tool. If online research is a viable option for you, search under "Medicaid long-term care for the elderly" for your state. Each state has different guidelines and regulations. New Mexico provides a Social Service Resource Directory, which provides a wealth of information and even the forms for applying for assistance.

I contacted the local state office of Human Services, and they put me in contact with a caseworker. I made an appointment and began gathering specific, factual information about my situation so I could make an informed decision. Most of these folks are very empathetic, knowledgeable, and helpful. They are aware of the difficult situation you're trying to cope with and the tough decisions you're facing. They're there to assist you, and they will support you during this trying time.

UNEXPECTED PAPERWORK

....

ROBERT HAD BEEN HOSPITALIZED AT the VA for only about two weeks when I received a letter from our insurance company stating that his doctor had requested an extension of his original discharge date of November 6. The determination of the insurance company was not to approve his physician's request. I had the right to appeal their decision.

I felt like I had just experienced an earthquake. My world wasn't very well glued together as it was, and now they were telling me they might release Robert from the hospital prior to his evaluations. But to where? He couldn't come home; he couldn't live on his own; the application for long-term care and Medicaid was not yet completed. Certainly they wouldn't just release him to the streets; he couldn't survive there.

I called Robert's social worker, Charles, at the VA. It was his job to arrange placement and follow-up care. I told him we were working as hard and as fast as we could to arrange for Robert's long-term care and safety, and I told him about the multiple agenda items.

We talked about Robert's behavior on the unit. Charles told me Robert was "a very complex person." I agreed and I shared some experiences from Robert's past. I emphasized the importance of their evaluations in our attempts to make appropriate decisions for Robert's future. He assured me they would do the testing that was necessary to make an adequate diagnosis of Robert's mental and physical capabilities to live independently and provide recommendations for his long-term care. I thanked Charles for his assistance and told him I would contact the insurance company.

I composed a letter to the insurance company stating the need for an extended stay, including the reasons why the original date of discharge didn't allow adequate time for Robert's stabilization *and* evaluation to be completed. I explained the importance of the evaluations: to establish the need for guardianship for financial matters and for treatment and medical care decisions, to determine his ability to live independently versus the need for long-term care, and to evaluate his ability to safely drive a car. The evaluations were necessary so that an appropriate placement for Robert could be made—a placement that would provide for his safety as well as the safety of others.

I wrote the letter in my best nursing-eeze, justifying the doctor's request. The insurance company finally approved his extended stay, so actual discharge didn't occur for an additional three weeks.

Thank God for my expertise in letter writing!

SPENDING DOWN

· ·

HAVE YOU EVER DREAMED OF winning the lottery or inheriting a large sum of money? Have you ever tried to figure out how you would spend that money? Most of us adopt a lifestyle that accommodates our income; as our income changes, our spending habits fluctuate accordingly.

For Robert and me, our main goal had been to accumulate as much savings as possible to ensure an adequate income for me in the event of his death. There would be no spousal benefits from his pension or from Social Security; my income would be based on *my* work history. I was a late bloomer to the work world, and my retirement income would be very small—well below the average Medicaid income level figures. We anticipated this, so once I started working as a nurse, at age fifty, we saved as much as we could to accumulate a supplemental income for me when I retired or was widowed.

Now Medicaid was requiring that we spend those funds. I needed to engage in a spending spree. Fun! Right? Just the contrary. It was stressful and frightening, and I was feeling like a victim of the system. I had worked for over twenty years to accumulate a nest egg, and now I had to get rid of it. And for the rest of my life, I would be limited to only dire necessities in my spending because of my lack of income. It wasn't fair. However, I had no choice if Robert was to get the care he needed and that I personally couldn't provide.

So I wrote a master spending plan. I was allowed to spend the money on the house and my vehicle. I decided to get new kitchen and laundry appliances, not because I needed them but because it seemed a wise investment. I wouldn't have the funds for replacements in the future. I got a new hot-water heater and also a system for recycling the hot water to help decrease my future utility bills.

I had concrete sidewalks laid on either side of the house and a concrete patio made behind the garage. Robert had had problems walking on the stones in these areas, and I figured I would probably have similar problems as I aged. I had a drainage system installed that would prevent heavy rains from running into the garage and creating problems with the items being stored there. I also had gutters installed on the eaves of the house.

I contracted to have the backyard divided by a picket fence. This would separate the rose garden from an area that would be mostly for Lady. She had a habit of racing from gate to gate in our backyard while "defending our borders." She created deep furrows in the ground and made walking on the backyard somewhat of an obstacle course. Someone could easily turn an ankle or fall. I also had a computerized watering system installed. This would ensure the roses would be watered even if I were on vacation.

Next I expanded my list to include decorating the inside of the house. When we expanded the living room, I had purchased a new couch and end tables, but we were still using our old couch for additional seating. I replaced that with two comfortable armchairs and an ottoman. I also wanted to get a new master bedroom suite; I had never had a new bedroom suite in my adult life. Charline and I shopped for one, but everything seemed so massive, unlike the rest of the house's furnishings. I finally decided to have my bedroom furniture refinished to look like new. I also purchased several pictures that I had seen earlier but didn't buy because I hadn't wanted to spend the money.

The rest of the items were less expensive but seemed like good investments, such as a queen-size bed for the guest room, foam mattress toppers, a cabinet for the bathroom, a recliner for the living room, and a small chair for the second bedroom.

My list was long, but it didn't include a vehicle change. I felt I should invest in a newer vehicle to replace my ten-year-old one. Logically, I should keep Robert's new car and sell my old one, but I felt that wasn't the best thing for me. When I couldn't make a decision, I decided to put the car issue on hold for a while.

We were nearing the time of Robert's release from the VA hospital. I had been in contact with his social worker and doctors during the past month, but I hadn't talked with Robert himself. I told his social worker that he couldn't come back to the house. I wouldn't live with him again.

Robert finally told his social worker that he would agree to be discharged to the Veterans Home in TorC. His discharge date was the Monday after Thanksgiving, November 27. His evaluations had been done the week before, and the paperwork stating the results would be sent with him to the Home. The VA staff didn't feel he was capable of living independently or of driving a car. His driver's license had expired on November 17 and would not be renewed.

I went to the Veterans Home to make the arrangements for his admission. I talked to the admissions specialist about our current personal and financial situation. I told her I was in the process of qualifying us for Medicaid and our target date was February 1. I also told her about our car situation. She suggested that I purchase Robert's car from our savings before I filled out the paperwork for his admission, thereby eliminating a long-term loan and spending down by that amount.

The next day I paid off the car loan from our saving account. Now I owned two cars.

A BITTERSWEET RETURN

· ·

ROBERT ARRIVED AT THE VETERANS Home on November 27, the Monday after Thanksgiving. He had been hospitalized for nearly seven weeks. He was very happy to be out of the hospital and back in familiar surroundings. Because he had spent a month at the Home in January, he knew the staff and many of the residents. They welcomed him wholeheartedly.

I went to the Home that morning and completed his admission paperwork. I also brought him some personal items and clothing. We had dinner together and talked about recent happenings in the family and in TorC. Yet our relationship was guarded; neither of us knew what to expect from the other. It was quite a contrast from the previous January admission day. That arrival had been filled with relief and joy, love, and hope for the future. Now there was doubt and uncertainty, distrust and defiance.

It's true that we had been physically separated for the last seven weeks, but sitting side by side in the same room, we were more distanced from each other than we had ever been in our twenty-four years of marriage. During that time, our relationship had been based on unconditional love and honesty, with mutual respect and trust, and a knowledge that no matter what happened, we would always be there for each other. Now it was different.

Robert was not a happy camper at the Veterans Home. He wanted to come back to our house to live, and he constantly threatened to walk out of the facility. When he was reminded that he was unable to walk for any distance, he said he would call a cab. When he said he wanted to come home to live, I reminded him I could no longer take care of him and that I didn't trust him anymore. He said he would to go a motel and hire someone to take care of him.

Around and around we all went; he talked to the social worker, to the doctor, to the nurses, and to his visitors. He wanted to leave, and he was determined to find a way. The administrator of the facility called a meeting to address the issue. She told me that the facility was not a prison, and residents were free to come and go as they chose. If he did attempt to leave, they couldn't restraint him. For his safety, it might be necessary, if the situation escalated, to transfer him to another type of facility.

I shared this information with Robert, along with reminding him that I had his power of attorney for health care. If he continued to be what they call a flight risk, I would have to consider a transfer to a state mental facility that was equipped to retain incapacitated people. I showed him the reports from his doctors at the VA, stating he wasn't capable of living independently or of driving a vehicle.

His reply was "They don't know what they're talking about." He didn't want to give up his feeling of control over himself, his ability to make his own decisions. That was understandable. He had become responsible for himself and making his own decisions at a very early age. It was hard for him to let that go—or even to change his thinking when there was a major disagreement. Dealing with Robert was like dealing with a two-year-old operating from a seventy-year-old's wealth of resourcefulness.

These constant disagreements were very trying and tiring for me. My visits to Robert usually left me in a deflated and dejected state of mind. I was visiting only three times a week, in contrast to the daily visits I'd made during his January admission. I felt he needed to have more time to bond with the other residents and to accept the facility's events and activities in order to feel at home there. I guess I needed to have more patience for that process.

I remember one particularly heartbreaking visit. It was only two weeks after his admission, on December 10, our twenty-fifth wedding anniversary. We had looked forward to celebrating that anniversary ever since our twentieth. The staff had told Robert they would have a special surprise for us and we were both excited.

That day I brought Robert an anniversary card, and we had dinner together. I wondered what he might have worked out with the staff as a surprise, but nothing special occurred. After dinner he told me he didn't think he could love me anymore if I continued to make him live in the Home. He said if I loved him, I would take him home. Since I wouldn't do that, I didn't love him—so, he didn't love me anymore either.

I told him it didn't work that way. You either love someone or you don't. You can't make it happen; you can't will it. It just happens. Once you love someone—*really* love that person—you'll always love him or her. That doesn't mean you can necessarily live together or be married; it doesn't mean you always like or condone that person's behavior or that you will always tolerate that behavior. Loving someone and accepting that person's behavior is not the same. We all have boundaries. Sometimes a loved one may cross those boundaries, and we can't accept that behavior. However, that doesn't mean we no longer love that person. It merely means we have to interact differently than we did before.

My bit of philosophy didn't "hack it" with Robert. He told me he wanted me to leave; he didn't want me to visit him anymore. As I left the dining room, I realized my words didn't hack it right then with me either. I felt—well, dejected and deflated are inadequate words for describing my feelings at the time. Tears started to well up in my eyes.

I headed for Robert's physical therapist's office. He took one look at me and asked what had happened. I told him briefly, and we talked a bit. Then he called Robert's social worker and escorted me to her office.

I told to her what had happened, and we talked for a while. I knew, logically, that Robert was still fighting for control. However, previously we had always fought fair. We never said hurtful things to each other when we were having a disagreement. We never attacked each other personally. We argued about the issue at hand and tried never to bring in other things that weren't directly related. Now it was different; now we seemed to be hurting each other. After talking with her, I felt better and went home with dry eyes.

The next morning, Robert called to say he was sorry for the things he'd said and that he hoped I would visit him again as soon as I could. He also said he loved me.

I replied, "I love you, too, Robert."

FYI Commentary

How do you explain the anger and negativity that so many nursing home residents have?

The specific answer to this question is as complex as each individual resident and the circumstances leading up to his or her admission. However, attitude is strongly influenced by the person's basic personality and worldview. Was he or she basically an optimist or a pessimist? Did he or she tend to look at life situations as half full or half empty? Did he or she usually adapt to new situations, seeing them as a way to learn and grow? Can he or she accept not always being in control? One's basic approach to life becomes much more pronounced and obvious in the elder years.

Most residents are grieving and are stuck in that process. Their statements reflect various stages of the grieving process. They're angry and depressed over their losses. (Anger and depression are two stages of the grieving process.) The lack of control over their life and their limited choices, feeling rejected or abandoned by family and society, and their admission to a long-term care facility are often perceived by them as a death sentence. You often hear comments like "It's a one-way door into here, and there's no chance of getting out." "My family doesn't want to be bothered with me anymore. They wanted to get me out of the way." Residents often feel useless and that life is over for them. These feelings and statements are related to the "poor me" stage of grieving.

Often there's a great deal of denial (another stage of grieving) regarding the extent of their impairments and their resulting limitations. "I don't need to be here. I can take care of myself. Just give me the chance." Often residents can't seem to accept their limitations, regardless of how obvious they may be to others. A resident might also make statements that reflect the bargaining stage of grief, such as, "If you really love me, you'll let me come home. If you don't, I won't love *you* anymore."

It's said that misery loves company, and residents often commiserate with each other. This tends to reinforce their negativity and contributes to the continuation of their anger. To further justify their feelings, they complain to each other about the food, staff, and their environment in general.

Robert verbalized all the above feelings and vacillated between the various stages. It wasn't until his level of function became extremely limited that he began to accept his situation. At that time, he didn't verbalize a positive attitude, but he did cease to express negative feelings and appeared to appreciate the care he was receiving.

Those individuals who make their own choice to become residents seem to have the most positive attitudes. They view their situation as half full and seem to appreciate the benefits of their environment. They participate more fully in the activities available and appear to enjoy themselves more. They report that their quality of life is good, and they are basically happy with things.

183

A WHIRLING DERVISH

· ·

WITH ROBERT'S ARRIVAL IN TORC, my life became even more complex. My visits to him were emotionally draining, and my agenda was mind boggling and physically demanding. There were trips to Las Cruces to buy furniture and furnishings to spend down our savings. There were multiple appointments with counselors, lawyers, doctors, caseworkers, contractors, and workers, and constant telephone conversations with their staff.

The decisions I had to make on a daily basis were seemingly endless: Do you want this color? Should it be this size or the smaller one? Do you prefer this model with these features or that one which, in some ways, is more efficient? It went on and on.

I normally take a long time to make decisions. I like to gather information from multiple sources before I decide, especially about things that are important for the long term and that involve spending large sums of money. But I had to make choices right away. There wasn't time to ponder or check every other option before deciding. It was yes or no—and *now*! I felt my life had become a whirling dervish spinning out of control, faster and faster, and I just couldn't keep up.

I was always tired and always cold. No matter how much sleep I got, I woke up tired. No matter how many clothes I layered on my body or how high I set the thermostat, I was cold. I finally went to see Dr. Spruce and voiced my complaints to her. When she ran blood tests, she discovered that my thyroid was no longer functioning properly, and I would need to start on medication to help correct the problem. I would need to take it for the rest of my life.

So I felt like I was falling apart physically, too. Would it never end?

PRACTICE MAKES PERFECT

· ·

THE OLD ADAGE "PRACTICE MAKES perfect" may or may not be true, but practice certainly promotes improvement. I became much better at making quick decisions. I changed my mindset. First I began to realize that most decisions don't have dire consequences. It makes little difference whether you choose A or B. I also learned to look for what I wanted or what appealed to me on sight—then check the price. If it was reasonably priced and I liked it, I'd buy it. It wasn't important if it was a few dollars cheaper across town. By the time I considered my time, energy, and gasoline costs, there was very little net difference between one store and another. Also, choosing a store that retailed items within your general price range automatically narrows your choices to items priced within your budget.

If I were purchasing appliances or items that might need servicing in the future, I looked for and chose the most dependable businesses available and with reputations for good follow-up service. When contracting for yard work, I chose someone whose work I had seen and who was a reliable, responsible worker. Sometimes a craftsperson has a portfolio showing his or her work. During an interview, it's sometimes important to listen to your gut feelings: if it feels like the two of you can work well together, you probably can. The opposite is also true.

So, on the basis of these guidelines, I proceeded to trust myself to make a right decision for me and not constantly second-guess myself. My attitude change helped a great deal to get me through the Medicaid spend-down process. I literally spent tens of thousands of dollars in less than six weeks. The nursing home costs for two months and four days totaled over $16,000 alone. I also lost large sums of money because of early withdrawal penalties from investment plans. However, I had no choice. To provide Robert with the lifelong care he needed, there was no other way.

FROM CHAOS TO ORDER

BY MID-DECEMBER, THE ITEMS ON my agenda were beginning to fall into place. The application for Medicaid had been filed. Robert had been admitted to the New Mexico State Veterans Home. I had the power of attorney and temporary guardianship paperwork for Robert that enabled me to secure needed documents and initiate changes for final approval for Medicaid. The evaluations had been completed, and the application papers for permanent guardianship were being drawn up. A court date for the hearing was being scheduled.

A lawyer who specialized in Medicaid regulations had been enlisted to prepare the paperwork for the income diversion trust. It would be initiated after we qualified for Medicaid. The spend-down process was underway and progressing well.

One major item on the agenda that I had been ignoring was the cars. Medicaid would allow me to have only one vehicle; I had two. I felt my 1997 Ford Taurus was too old to keep for the rest of my life. But the 2006 Taurus represented frustrations and negativity, and it symbolized the anger I felt toward my present situation. It also represented feelings of being victimized, feelings of insecurity and helplessness. Neither car seemed an acceptable choice for the future. I needed to move forward.

I decided I would trade them both in for a used vehicle of *my* choice. It was December, and the '07 models would be on the lot. I was hopeful that I could find a used '06 that was still under warranty. I also decided to buy an extended warranty to reduce any repair costs. The car and its warranty would be part of my spend-down process, too.

I asked Charline to go with me to look at cars, because I wanted some moral support. She drove, and I talked with Doug, the owner at the Chevrolet dealership. (Of course, I wanted nothing to do with Turtleback Motors.) I had talked to Doug back in October. He had been made aware of parts of my situation and had promised to cooperate if Robert showed up to purchase a car.

Doug told me Robert had been there wanting to buy a car. He had arrived by taxi and spent all afternoon at the dealership, trying to negotiate a sale. Doug had priced the available cars out of Robert's price range. When Robert got agitated, Doug offered to give him a ride home. It was the next day that Robert went to Turtleback Motors and purchased the car.

I explained to Doug what had happened with Turtleback Motors and what I wanted to do now with the two vehicles. He showed me several cars, but I didn't see one that I liked. Then I spotted a red Impala. It was a four-door with leather seats, a sunroof, and a spoiler on the trunk. It was a 2006 and still under warranty. There was a computerized system for monitoring every function of the vehicle. It was one awesome car. As it turned out, it was Doug's car, but also the only red vehicle on the lot. Doug decided it was for sale; he said he usually traded cars each year when the new models came out, and it was that time of year.

We talked finances and warranties. He gave me the Blue Book trade-in values for my vehicles, and I said I wanted to purchase an extended warranty. When I left the dealership, I had completed the initial paperwork to purchase the Impala. Doug said he would have his staff wash, wax, and detail it for me, and I could pick it up the next afternoon.

So the next afternoon Charline drove one of my cars, and I followed her in the other. I completed the final paperwork, and we traded keys and vehicles. Doug gave me a quick lesson on the computer system and assured me it was just fine to come in for more services if I needed them.

It was December 15, and I had just bought myself the most expensive Christmas present of my life and the first vehicle I had ever purchased by myself. It was so deluxe; it had everything on it. I felt very special driving home that afternoon.

When I woke up the next morning, I went straight to the garage. I looked at my car. What had I done? I didn't need a car like that; I didn't need leather seats or a sunroof. It was so much more car than I needed. My first thought was *I must return it. I have spent too much money!*

I called Charline and told her I thought I'd made a mistake. I'd gotten caught up in the moment. I didn't need that deluxe a vehicle. She listened for a bit and then firmly said, "You deserve that car! After what you've been through, you deserve it. Just enjoy it. You've earned it."

Once we finished talking, I went back out to the garage. I sat in the car. I played the radio, adjusted the seats, and ran through the computer checks and monitoring systems. I opened and closed the sunroof. I got out and examined the trunk and the spoiler. I looked at the color. It was a deep red with white striping along the sides. It was a beautiful car!

I went into the house and got one of my CDs. I got back into the driver's seat, inserted the CD, and just sat there, listening to the music. The sound system was great. Everything felt good; it felt right. I loved my new car—my new red Impala.

Merry Christmas, Lee!

GONE BUT NOT FORGOTTEN

I NO LONGER HAD ROBERT'S blue '06 Taurus. I no longer saw it on a daily basis, sitting in my driveway. I had traded it in for my wonderful red Impala. The blue Taurus was gone.

However, my anger toward Turtleback Motors was still with me. I'd worked on my complaint claim to the New Mexico Attorney General for some time. On December 19, 2006, I'd mailed it to the Consumer Protection Agency of the Attorney General's office. I included my account of the circumstances leading up to the sale of the car to Robert, his hospitalization, and my dilemma with Turtleback Motors.

On January 2, 2007, I received a reply from their staff. They said they used the mediation process to resolve claims, and they would contact Turtleback Motors in Socorro and explain the process to them. I wasn't to contact Turtleback Motors directly; their office would make the contacts between the two parties.

Meanwhile, I had decided to publish my story in the local newspaper in the "Letters to the Editor" section. My son had cautioned me that I shouldn't say anything that could be deemed libelous. I contacted my backdoor neighbor, Marty, who was a retired judge and asked if he would read the letter and check it for libelous content. After he had read it, he told me he found no problems with my account and thought it was a fine letter. I asked him if I had a case. He said he felt my letter would allow me to "vent my spleen," but probably nothing more would come of it. I told him that might be enough to make me feel better about the situation and to let it go. "Then print it," he said.

I took the letter to the two local newspapers. One editor refused to publish it: he said he feared it might cause his paper to be sued. I told him I'd checked that out and I'd pay to have the article printed in his paper. He still refused to print it.

I went to the other newspaper office. The editor said she would check with their lawyer and print the letter if he approved it. It was longer than the free space for "Letters to the Editor," so I would have to pay for the extra words. She called the next day saying their lawyer had approved its publication. That afternoon I paid, and it was published the following week, January 3. (Our local papers are weekly publications.)

I received numerous telephone calls from strangers regarding the letter; they were all supportive. Many said they wouldn't buy another car from Turtleback Motors. Some called to sympathize, some to wish me well in my struggle.

On January 30, I received a copy of Charles Marshall's response to the claim that I had filed with the Attorney

General's Office. That reply to my claim was very weak. On February 13, the lawyer from the Attorney General's Office called to ask if I wished to pursue my claim. He said their office acted only as mediators in an attempt to resolve issues. If I wished to pursue my claim, I would need to secure a lawyer and sue Turtleback Motors.

I told him I didn't wish to pursue my claim. Publishing my story had been therapeutic for me. The responses from the community had helped to dissipate my anger. "Venting my spleen" had been good for my soul. I had let it go.

FYI Commentary

What does the phrase "Let go and let God" mean?

I first heard this phrase while I worked on the substance abuse unit at a VA hospital. It's used in the context of working with patients in the twelve-step program recommended for recovering addicts. The phrase is a tool to help them cope with the anger, frustration, and negative feelings that surface once they've become drug-free. They try to learn to let go of their negative feelings from the past and give them to their Higher Power, or whatever name they might choose. (Universe, Source, Creator, and God are frequently used names.)

The goal is to seek forgiveness from those they have wronged and to forgive those they perceive have wronged them and, finally, to forgive themselves. They attempt to let go of their anger and let God deal with the injustices of this world. The focus is on forgiveness and moving on, on having no more thoughts of getting even or holding a grudge. You "let God" be the judge and the jury. You recognize that the negative feelings you harbor are like a cancer that eats at you and prevents you from loving yourself and others. Completing these steps helps you to be able to move on and achieve a more productive and fulfilling life. It is a beautiful concept and a catchy slogan.

However, it can be an extremely difficult and painful process that may take years to actually accomplish. Angry feelings are usually the result of feeling wronged—not having been treated fairly and with the respect and love you feel you deserve—by another person, group, or system. You feel your trust has been betrayed. You feel you've been victimized (unfairly taken advantage of). The more meaningful this person is or was in your life and the longer the negative situation lasted, the deeper and sharper the resulting pain is and the more difficult it is to let the anger go and release the pain.

Over my lifetime, I've finally developed a worldview that helps me to forgive and let the anger go. I realize that it's hurting only me, not the target of my anger. My anger prevents me from moving on and being a free spirit and a loving and positive person. The events in my story—the anger I felt toward Turtleback Motors, having to spend my life savings, trying to cope with Robert's irrational behaviors, and my perceived powerlessness in these situations—were difficult to resolve. However, events in my earlier life— issues with my parents and with my first husband—were much more difficult to let go of. The process took years to accomplish and continually needs to be honed.

Learning how to be assertive and becoming my own person were tasks I had to master before I could totally "let go and let God." Once accomplished, there was a wonderful feeling of relief and a freeing of my self to move forward and live in the present. To "let go and let God" is a *learned* process, and I would say that I was a very slow learner.

NEW YEAR, NEW BEGINNINGS

THE YEAR 2007 DAWNED—AND WITH it many changes were initiated. By January 12 our spend-down was completed. Robert's total resources were less than $2,000. The State of New Mexico allowed a spousal transfer of up to $31,290. Our total resources were now under this amount; therefore, we met the financial eligibility requirements of Medicaid. We were approved for Medicaid funds for institutional nursing home care to begin February 1.

On February 9, the Robert Hildebrandt Income Diversion Trust was initiated. Robert's entire pension would be deposited into that account. The trustee would write the checks for Robert's medical care, health care insurance, spousal income support, and specific administrative costs. The remainder of his monthly pension monies over $1,809 would be left to accumulate in the trust. Upon his death, they would go to Medicaid for partial payment of his total care costs while on Medicaid. I was made the trustee of the trust account. It was my responsibility to disperse the monies appropriately and keep monthly records of the account activities.

These two events completed our requirements for Medicaid funding. Robert's medical care was ensured for the rest of his lifetime. What a relief! I would have one year to complete the paperwork for the spousal transfer of any jointly held resources to my name only. There would be a yearly review to monitor any changes that may have occurred.

The only remaining item on my agenda list was our court date for the permanent guardianship hearing. I was scheduled for February 5. This is a complex procedure designed to protect the rights and freedoms of the individual whose competency is in question. It's a formal court procedure presided over by a judge. A lawyer represents each side. There are witnesses called and evidence submitted by both sides to determine the need for a guardian and, if needed, the appointment of a guardian.

Robert and I were each present and represented by a lawyer. Robert had been transported to the courtroom in a wheelchair, accompanied by a nursing assistant from the Home. He and his lawyer were seated on one side of the room. I was seated across the room with my lawyer.

Several weeks earlier, a social worker had interviewed each of us to collect information regarding the circumstances of the case. She had also contacted Robert's children by letter, explaining the proceedings and asking for their input related to Robert's prior mental status and behaviors and any objections they might have to me becoming his guardian.

Her report and the evaluations by the VA hospital doctors were submitted as evidence. The medical director of the New Mexico State Veterans Home testified regarding his assessment of Robert's capacities to function independently. All the evidence presented confirmed his need for a guardian. When questioned, Robert had no rebuttal.

The paperwork for my request to be appointed guardian was submitted. He was asked if he had any objections to my appointment as his guardian. He replied, "She's always looked out for me and in my best interest. No reason to change things now." The judge stamped the papers, and the hearing was over.

The nursing assistant escorted Robert out of the courtroom. My lawyer told me to wait with him so I could obtain the official stamped documents for the proceedings. The entire process took less than half an hour.

AN AWESOME ROLE

As I DROVE HOME AFTER the proceedings, I pondered my official new role. It was awesome to think about. I had complete control over another person's life—another adult person. As a parent, I had played that role, but it was different—more natural, maybe. Babies are born totally dependent on their caregivers, and it follows that you have to make all the decisions for and about these small beings in their early years.

However, this was an adult person who had been fully functional for years. He had been a good decision maker and had been one of my best resources when I had a problem to solve. Now I would be making all the major decisions for him. What strange twists and turns we take along life's path.

Sitting across the courtroom from Robert was the most public display of adversarial behavior I had ever participated in. I felt like a vulture stripping its prey of all its outward trappings, laying the body open to the public eye for all to see. I had stripped Robert of his right to control his life choices, and I had done it publicly, showing the whole world his frailties and weaknesses. What kind of monster was I?

As I changed my clothes, I tried to change my thinking. The scenario in my mind was playing like this: Robert's judgment ability was impaired. It was often similar to that of my children when they were two-year-old toddlers. They definitely needed a guardian at that time to keep them safe and healthy. Now Robert needed a guardian to keep him safe and healthy. If I hadn't intervened with my children, I would have been charged with child abuse or child neglect. Now I had to intervene for Robert's sake. I had assumed my responsibility as a parent to maintain the safety and well-being of my children because I loved them and they needed you. I was now assuming my responsibility as a mate, best friend, and lover to maintain the safety and well-being of my husband because I loved him and he needed me. Children don't always like the boundaries that we set, and Robert doesn't either, but they are necessary. I knew my role wasn't that of a monster. It was that of a caretaker and caregiver— and I had to give tough love. It's not an easy role to carry out.

After fortifying myself with the pep talk, I drove myself to the nursing home to have dinner with Robert. Our interaction was somewhat strained when I first got there. He was very aware of what had transpired in the courtroom that morning—and he didn't like it. However, I got the impression that, at some level, he knew he couldn't cope with things the way he used to and that he needed help. But more importantly, he could claim that he was being compelled by the court to *accept help;* the deck had been stacked against him. Like it or not, he *had to* accept his fate. It was his way of being able to save face.

Later, as we sat playing bingo, I reached over to hold his hand. Softly I said, "I love you. You know that, right?"

"Yes," he replied. "I know you do."

CLEARING THE DESK

. . . .

ONCE ROBERT WAS DECLARED LEGALLY incapacitated and I was appointed his guardian and conservator, I needed to complete the last task of Medicaid's long list of requirements. I needed to transfer all our currently jointly owned assets to my name only—mainly, the house and the remaining savings annuity. I also needed to become the owner of Robert's life insurance policies. I needed to take his name off as the beneficiary of my life insurance, and I needed to initiate a new will. Also, our revocable living trust had to be revoked. Any monies Robert had in excess of $2,000 would belong to Medicaid. Robert could virtually own nothing and could inherit nothing. Also I needed to become the payee for his Civil Service pension so I could execute any changes as they became necessary.

There were multiple phone calls and letters to request the needed paperwork to make these changes. There were forms to complete and return along with proof of my guardianship status and, in some cases, proof of our marriage. Once the resources were all transferred to my name, I needed to make out a new will naming new beneficiaries. My old will named Robert as my beneficiary, and if I were to precede him in death, Medicaid would ultimately become the beneficiary of any and all of my assets.

It was a lengthy process to contact the various agencies, fill out and return their paperwork, and then wait for confirmation that everything was properly completed. However, it was very fulfilling to close each file, remove it from my dining-room table, and place it in the filing cabinet in the study. (These files had been on my table since October—four months.)

At last my mountain of paperwork was gone and my life could begin to take a new path—one of fewer deadlines, shorter lists, and less anxiety, confusion, and stress. Perhaps I could even consider a vacation, visit my kids and grandkids. Just the thoughts of that made me feel wonderful—like I had suddenly been granted a pardon and released from prison.

REST, RELAXATION, AND ROUTINE

I SCHEDULED MY VACATION FOR two weeks in Florida during April. I had not seen any of my children for nearly two years—five years since I'd last seen my grandchildren. What a wonderful time I had! I was royally wined and dined and entertained by everyone. The children were working weekdays, so I had time to see several of my retired friends and also had lunch with the doctor I'd worked with at the VA hospital in Gainesville. I spent three days with my older sister and her husband. I also visited the ocean and walked along the beach. I hadn't seen the Atlantic or Gulf waters for five years. I love the ocean and the beach, so this was a special treat.

I laughed and hugged; reminisced; shared feelings, thoughts, and ideas; and caught up on some of the news of my friends. I overate and drank my fill, stayed up late, and slept in. I began to feel like a real person again—a person with a zest for living. I was *living*—not just surviving, as I had been doing for the last two years. As with all vacations, it came to an end, but it had been *so* special and *so* exhilarating. My batteries were recharged.

When I got back to TorC, I felt relaxed and ready to resume some of the activities I used to enjoy before Robert became ill. I started line dancing again. I went to my favorite bookstore for coffee and a scone. I did yard work and nurtured my garden. I went swimming and joined the water aerobics class. I walked and played with Lady. I went to Red Hats and shopped in Las Cruces.

I also visited Robert at least three times a week and usually spent most of the day with him. I'd arrive at noon, have dinner with him, spend the afternoon, have supper, and leave when he went to bed in the evening. I would bring Robert, the residents, and the staff flowers from the garden. I brought Robert treats from my kitchen, too; he liked my cole slaw better than what they served in the dining room. I also brought his favorite cookies and various snacks. The Home provided quite a variety of food and snacks, but he enjoyed having me bring things, and I enjoyed doing it.

We each had established a routine that seemed to work. He was adapting to life at the Home, and I was adapting to living alone. He played the piano for himself and the other residents, went to physical therapy, and attended some of the many activities provided by the Home to keep residents stimulated and active. We went to bingo and played cards and pool. There were always holiday celebrations, cookouts, dances, and movies. Robert didn't choose to participate in many of the events, but when I was there I could often get him to give things a try.

Periodically, he would get very negative about having to live at the Home and try to convince me that he could live on his own. He had a variety of options he would present: living in our garage, in a trailer in the back yard, in a one-room apartment. He was sure he could manage by himself. We would discuss these ideas, and I would tell him that if he really wanted to be able to live outside the Home, he would need to work on strengthening his muscles to improve his abilities to take care of himself on a daily basis—bathing, dressing, toileting, eating, and exercising. Also, I encouraged him to participate in activities to keep his mind active. He would make an effort to be more independent for a short time (at least an hour or so), but he couldn't sustain it for long.

Robert's ability to ambulate, even with assistive devices, was declining. His legs just weren't working much anymore. The physical therapy department found him a motorized scooter to use, and he was delighted. He could "drive" again, and he could readily get from his room to anyplace in the facility. The scooter gave him increased independence, and that added a great deal of quality to his life. It gave him some hope.

Life had become very different for each of us, but we were slowly adjusting to the changes. We had each developed a routine, and even though it may not have been our preferred choice, it was better than the chaos and stress that had preceded it.

ROUTINE OR RUT?

· ·

AT FIRST MY ROUTINE WAS a pleasant change from the chaos and stress of my mountain of paperwork and its accompanying agenda. That had been such an overwhelming challenge. Once that was over, it was another challenge to establish some semblance of stability in my life again, in spite of its many recent changes.

I had been on a Medicaid budget for about five months. It was like a game to me to be able to live within my reduced budget; I needed to know that I could manage solely on my own income. It was also necessary. With the bulk of my savings gone, there were no supplemental funds to augment my monthly income. I couldn't spend what monies I had been allowed to keep; they must be held for emergencies only. I put myself on an itemized allowance to accommodate the fixed costs. I cut my utility bills as much as I could. I was very careful about eating out and not buying anything that wasn't really needed. I proved to myself that I could do it; I could make it work.

Spring had morphed into summer. The yard work was on autopilot until fall. Charline had left for a two-month visit with her sister in Michigan. It was hot—very hot. Many of my friends were vacationing in cooler parts of the country. I watched TV. I read. I visited Robert. I swam and line danced. I had my routine.

I was surviving, and things weren't bad, yet I had emptiness inside me. I felt unfulfilled, like my life had no purpose. One day an invitation came. It was to the wedding of my son John's stepdaughter in San Francisco. It wasn't until October, but they needed a head count to reserve the reception site. I replied, "I will not attend." Several weeks later, John, called me to chat and asked if the reason I had declined was because of money. I admitted I didn't see how I could fit it into my budget. He said he wanted me to be there to help them celebrate. He would send me the money for airfare and any other expenses I might have. I thanked him and said I'd plan on being there.

I started seriously considering my situation—my budget, my lifestyle, all of it—and I decided I needed to go back to work. It had been over four years since I had worked, but I still had an active nursing license. However, it would expire in November. To keep it active, I would need to be working and also complete some courses before it expired.

I checked the newspaper and called several facilities to find a position. I had several interviews that resulted in job offers, but I didn't feel they were a good fit for me. I didn't want to work nights, and I wanted to work part time.

A former colleague from the Behavioral Health Clinic offered to create a job for me, but I would need to audit his college course on a sophisticated psychological testing tool to qualify for the position. It would mean driving 150 miles twice a week to attend an evening class. I would have to drive back alone late at night or stay in a hotel overnight and drive home the next day. I was seriously considering accepting this job when I had an interview for a job with hospice patients.

I had always wanted to be involved with hospice care—long before I had become a nurse. I wholly support the hospice concepts and principles. I went for the job interview and had instant rapport with the director of the program. I was offered the job on the spot. I'd be working three days a week in a healthcare facility, and making home visits.

I told the director, Dottie, that I hadn't been a bedside nurse for over twenty years. She said, "Once a nurse, always a nurse. It will all come back to you again. It's the psych background that makes you most valuable for the position. They can't teach you that in nursing school. We have a one-month orientation period. You'll be ready when you start working on your own."

Her words were very reassuring to me. I accepted the job, proud to become part of the hospice mission. I was to start in one week, September 4—the day after Labor Day. In the meantime, I had to get clearance, be fingerprinted, have a physical exam, take a TB test, and meet other employment requirements before the holiday weekend.

When I got home that afternoon, I sat down with a cup of coffee and relived the interview in my mind. What was I doing? I was seventy-one years old, and I hadn't done hands-on care for a quarter of a century. Now I was going to make home health visits and be caring for terminal people. I thought I must be crazy.

When I had expressed my doubts to Dottie, she seemed confident I could handle the responsibilities of the job. She had been working in hospice for many years; I figured she should know what she was talking about. I was excited and fearful—and anxious to tell Robert. He had always been so supportive of me in my career and had always been my biggest cheerleader. I had told him earlier that I needed to find a job because I could make it on my income alone but just barely. I needed to have more of a cushion to allow for occasional treats or splurges.

The next day I told Robert about the interview, about Dottie, about my doubts and fears—everything I could remember. He was very happy for me; he knew how I felt about the hospice movement. We had contributed to the building fund in Gainesville when they were seeking support to build a freestanding hospice facility there, and we had been actively involved with it becoming a reality. He thought I would make a perfect hospice nurse. I welcomed his words of reassurance.

Routine or rut? The question had now become moot.

ORIENTATION

. . . .

REENTERING THE WORKFORCE WAS STRESSFUL. I hadn't worked in a medical care setting for almost ten years. I felt very much out of the loop. However, my colleagues were supportive of and very patient with their new elderly recruit. Another nurse and I would be working as a team to care for the hospice patients. As it turned out, we already knew each other from previous participation in various community events.

There were many practices and procedures to learn and lots of paperwork to become familiar with. There were many new names and faces to learn. I also was no longer used to an eight-to-five workday. Thank goodness it was only three days a week.

My preceptor nurse was a recent RN graduate and young enough to be my granddaughter. She was very good at her work, and we got along well. I shadowed her for about two weeks. She introduced me to the patients and their families; I learned where they lived and their social and medical history; I observed what she did and how she did it; I learned what paperwork needed to be completed for each procedure.

Then we slowly changed roles, and she shadowed me. I learned to complete the routine paperwork, do admissions, manage medications, and deal with the various doctors, pharmacies, and agencies involved. I had to become certified by the State of New Mexico Office of the Medical Investigator as a hospice deputy medical investigator designate. This certification allowed me to declare a client deceased, notify the attending physician, and fill out the necessary paperwork so the body could be transported to a funeral home.

There was a lot of information and learning packed into that orientation month. I adapted slowly to being a working girl once again. Actually, it was exhilarating to be working with professional colleagues again; it gave me a new sense of worth and identity. And it was fulfilling and rewarding to be part of the hospice team. Needless to say, it was also rewarding to receive my first paycheck and to I called Marla to tell her I was working and no longer eligible for the Medicaid Community Spouse Maintenance Allowance monies. My income exceeded the guidelines.

With the added income, I felt much more secure. If the house had a plumbing problem, I could afford to have it fixed. If I wanted to go to a family celebration, I could attend and pay my own way. I planned to continue to live on my former budget as much as possible and to save the majority of my employment monies to build a cushion for extras—things that might not qualify for my survival list but that were important for ensuring a minimal quality of life.

As the weeks passed, I developed a comfortable routine balancing work time, visiting Robert, leisure activities, and time spent with friends. My work experiences were constantly changing. I had established a routine, but it certainly wasn't a rut.

WEDDING BELLS

· ·

TIME SEEMED TO PASS RAPIDLY. Soon it was mid-October, and I was on a plane to San Francisco. It was Thursday, and the wedding was early Saturday afternoon. I would be staying with my daughter and her significant other until Sunday, when they had to fly back to Florida. They had rented an apartment close to John's house for the weekend.

I hadn't seen Debbie and Sean since April, and it was fun to see them again. On Friday morning Deb and I went grocery shopping, and in the afternoon we took the streetcar downtown and went shopping there. The weather was mild, and we spent some quality girl time together.

That evening was the rehearsal dinner. It was organized chaos, with people from different parts of the country arriving at different times, many of them meeting for the first time. There was food, drinks, jokes, laughter, and lots of noise. A good time was had by all.

As we walked back to the apartment, I was suddenly very tired. I had been battling a cold for several weeks and thought it was gone. However, with the added excitement and stress of traveling, it had resurfaced. I was coughing, very congested, and feeling somewhat fatigued. I bid the young couple goodnight and hoped I'd be feeling better in the morning.

We had to be ready by nine thirty Saturday morning to ride to the wedding site—a lighthouse on the Pacific coast about an hour from the city. John had arranged to have guests without a car shuttled to the site. The wedding was not until one, but we were with the wedding party, and the bride and attendants needed time to prepare for the ceremony. The California sun shone brightly, but the coastal winds were blowing, and the weather was cool and damp. We walked around the area and then sat outside in the guest area and visited until the ceremony began—about two hours later.

The bride was beautiful. The ceremony was lovely. A photographer took hundreds of pictures. We left the site to attend the reception at about three thirty. It was held in the clubhouse of the Presidio Golf Course. There was food, drinks, music, dancing, hugs, laughter, picture taking, conversation—it was a lovely evening. We got back to the apartment about ten that night. Deb and Sean decided to enjoy some of the night scenes of San Francisco, but I went directly to bed. I was exhausted.

I hacked and coughed all night, so I didn't sleep well at all. I woke up in a sweat several times. I was congested, and my cough had become persistent. I knew my cold was getting worse—much worse. In the last five years, I'd had pneumonia twice. I'd gotten the pneumonia shot after the second time and had been fine for the last three years. However, being in the cool, moist ocean air for nearly five hours had made my existing cold more serious. I was concerned.

We all met for breakfast at a nearby café on Sunday morning. Most of the group was returning home that day, but I was staying with my granddaughter, Andrea, until Wednesday morning. Her apartment was next door to John's house. After breakfast, we went back to Deb's place. Deb and Sean left for the airport, and John and I walked my luggage, etc., to his house a couple of blocks away.

We were about halfway there when I told John I needed to stop and rest. I told him about my cold and that it was getting significantly worse. He apologized to me for not noticing that I didn't feel well. I said he had been very preoccupied with the wedding and rightfully so, and that I hadn't felt really bad until that morning.

He said, "You know, Mom, I forget how old you really are. You always seem so young to me." I thanked him for the compliment but said I was feeling very old, very tired, and feverish. I told him I thought I needed some antibiotics and asked if he had a doctor I could get a prescription from. He said he would call a friend at the club who was a doctor.

When we got to Andrea's apartment, I said I needed to rest for a while. I slept for a couple of hours. When I awoke, I was feverish again. Andrea and I went next door to look at the wedding pictures from the day before. The bride was there to identify people we didn't recognize. The bride and groom weren't leaving on their honeymoon trip until the next weekend—after all the out-of-town guests had left. The groom was from New Jersey, and his friends and relatives had traveled a long distance for his wedding. The couple wanted to spend as much time with them as they could while they were on the West Coast.

I enjoyed looking at the wedding and reception pictures. Disposable cameras had been provided at each table at the reception, so guests could take pictures at will. They probably had at least one photo of each guest attending. After we were finished with the pictures, John told me he had talked with his doctor friend. He wouldn't prescribe antibiotics for me without examining me first. He suggested that John take me to the nearby hospital emergency room. I said that would be fine. My insurance would cover it, and I didn't feel I should let treatment wait until Thursday or Friday, when I arrived back home.

John and I went to the ER. I had an X-ray, was examined by the doctor, and he prescribed an antibiotic; I had acute bronchitis. I started taking the medication that evening. I slept much better that night. I also slept much of the next day. By Tuesday I was a little less fatigued and no longer feverish. I got a good night's sleep on Tuesday night, and Andrea took me to the airport on Wednesday morning.

My flight to El Paso was short, and I slept the entire way. The ride from the airport to Las Cruces and then to TorC was longer than my entire flight time. I arrived home Wednesday evening a very weary traveler. I was supposed to work Thursday, Friday, and Saturday, but I called Dottie and related what had happened. I spent the rest of the week trying to fight off any remaining cold germs and regain my strength.

I reported for work on Monday morning feeling very much better.

ONE FALSE MOVE

. . . .

I WAS BEGINNING TO ACQUIRE a feeling of mastery in the workplace. I knew what to do; I knew how to do it; I knew how and where to document it. This made work more enjoyable and allowed me to focus on interacting with my patients, their families, and my workmates. I began to enjoy my time at work.

Because of my work schedule, I was able to see Robert only twice a week. He had adjusted somewhat to the Veterans Home environment but still wasn't happy to be there. Also, his health was slowly declining. He was becoming more dependent on staff for assistance with his daily activities and care. It became more difficult for him to operate his motorized scooter. It was a side-access style, and he was having problems transferring to and from it.

The physical therapy staff sent him to the VA hospital in Albuquerque to be fitted for a front-access vehicle designed to accommodate his large frame. In the meantime, they took his other scooter away, feeling it was no longer safe for him to use. His new mode of transportation was a standard wheelchair. He wasn't happy about this at all, but he did have the new chair to look forward to. In general, things seemed to be running smoothly.

Thanksgiving was a four-day holiday, and I wasn't scheduled to work. I spent Thursday visiting Robert. I decided that Friday would be a great time to catch up on some of my housekeeping chores. The weather had turned cold, and I was attempting to connect the controls for the electric blanket. I couldn't reach them, so I tried to move the king-size bed out from the wall for better access. I only needed to move it a couple of inches, and I thought, *I should be able to do that.*

I'm a nurse, and one of the first things you learn in nursing school is the importance of good body mechanics. Many nurses are forced to go on disability because of back injuries that occur in the workplace, usually the result of using poor body mechanics. I knew what to do; I had been trained to safely lift and transfer patients, to pick up and carry heavy objects, to push heavy equipment, etc. Also, nurses are trained to assess a situation and decide when to call for assistance or to use assistive devices.

Obviously my training didn't transfer to the home scene that morning. Without thinking, I just bent down and tried to pull the bed away from the wall. It moved a couple of inches, enough for me to reach and connect the controls. As soon as I tried to straighten up, I realized what I'd done. There was no real sharp pain, but I felt like I had twisted something in my back.

Later in the day, I felt pain as I got up from sitting. At bedtime it was difficult to find a position that felt comfortable. I woke up in the middle of the night in pain. On a scale of one to ten, it was a five. I took a couple of aspirins and went back to sleep. I was able to sleep for a couple of hours and then awoke again. Now the pain was a seven. I just couldn't get comfortable, so I got up.

After two more aspirin, I went out to the living room and lay in the recliner. When I awoke in the morning, the pain was again a seven or eight. When I changed positions, it got worse. When I found a pain-free position and sat very still, I could get some relief. Movement meant pain.

I called Robert and told him what had happened. I had planned to visit him that day but told him I thought I should stay home. I told him that if I felt better the next day, I would try to visit him then.

I sat in the recliner all day, getting up only to go to the bathroom and to eat, though I had little or no appetite. I had nothing but over-the-counter pain medications in the house. Aspirin wasn't helping, so I decided to switch to ibuprofen and took a larger-than-usual dose. Then I got out my heating pad and sat with it against my back. It provided some relief, but I was still in constant pain.

I spent Saturday and Sunday in the recliner, including the night hours. I watched TV and slept and tried to move as little as possible. Since it was a holiday weekend, the clinic was closed; I'd have to just tough it out until Monday.

On Monday morning, I called Dr. Spruce's clinic. I was told she was on vacation. Another doctor was seeing her patients, but it would be mid afternoon before he could see me. I called Dottie, told her my problem, and said I would contact her after I'd seen the doctor. I called a friend, and she said she would drive me to the clinic.

My appointment was for three o'clock that afternoon. The doctor listened to my complaint and prescribed a muscle relaxant, a narcotic pain medication, and a potent nonnarcotic pain medication. I was given an injection in my buttocks for more immediate pain relief. He said I probably wouldn't feel well enough to work at all that week and recommended that I plan to rest and let my back heal.

I relayed that message to Dottie and told her I would keep her informed about my progress. I spent the next couple of days in my recliner. Toward the end of the week, I was feeling much better. I was no longer taking the narcotic medications and was able to go for long periods during the day without any meds at all. However, I still needed medication to sleep at night. By the weekend, I was pretty much pain-free and planned to go to work on Monday.

Monday morning came, and I reported for work. I had planned my work schedule to favor my back, seeing only the patients in the nursing home. It would require less physical exertion, less driving, and I could pace myself better. I took everything slowly and used every technique I knew to protect my back. I raised the beds so I wouldn't need to bend over to reach the patients; I was careful to turn my whole body—not twisting at the waist; I scheduled the patients who required the least amount of care first; I planned to take more frequent breaks than I normally would so I could be off my feet for short intervals.

I saw the first two patients, and everything seemed to be going well. I was assessing my third patient when it felt like something in my back snapped. The pain was excruciating!

I quickly finished with my patient and walked back to the office. The pain seemed unbearable. I had tears in my eyes and could barely speak. On a scale of one to ten, my pain was a fifteen.

As I came through the door, Dottie saw me, put me into one of the wheeled office chairs, and rolled me across the hall to the physical therapy department. The pain was in my back where it had been the previous week, but now it also extended down my right leg all the way into my toes. They laid me on one of their treatment beds and applied heat. Then the therapist manipulated my back and right leg. That hurt as much as my back was hurting. Once I could stand up, she put a back brace on me. I felt better, but I was still in a great deal of pain. My pain was maybe a nine.

Dottie drove me home in my car, and another colleague followed to take her back to the office. I thanked her for all her help and went into the house. As I entered the living room, I suddenly felt very alone and frightened. I had been very positive about my situation when I had injured my back. I knew what I had done, what had caused my back to hurt. I had felt that if I took the medications, rested to let my back heal, and was very careful with my activities and body movements, I would be as good as new in a short time. I had thought of my situation as having an unplanned, forced vacation; catching up on my TV watching; having a short time-out. I had gotten better, and I had felt good when I went to work that morning. I had tried to plan as idyllic a work situation as possible and do everything right to protect my back.

But look what had happened to me! I couldn't even complete two hours of work. The pain had been so intense—so much worse than the last time. What if I could no longer work? What if the pain became chronic? I lived alone, so what if I could no longer take care of myself? Would I have to spend the rest of my life in a recliner, dependent on a caretaker?

My thoughts were racing and wouldn't stop. I didn't have any answers, only doubts and fears. And the pain remained intense and constant. I had some narcotic pain medications left from the previous week, so I took a dose. I changed out of my work clothes, turned on the TV, connected my heating pad, sank into my recliner, and soon fell into a drugged sleep.

The next morning I called the clinic. Dr. Spruce was still on vacation, and I made an appointment to see the doctor servicing her practice. I called Charline to tell her what had happened in the last week or so. She had been visiting her daughter for the Thanksgiving holiday and was back home. She said she would take me to the clinic and help me in any other way she could.

I saw the doctor on duty at the clinic. It wasn't the man I had seen the week before, but he prescribed the same meds and treatments as before. He also said I should make a follow-up appointment with Dr. Spruce as soon as she returned.

I spent the next ten days at home, resting and trying to take care of myself. It was pretty much a repeat of the prior week, but I wasn't as optimistic about the outcome as I had been before. This time around, the pain in my back seemed to lessen quickly, but the pain in my right leg from groin to knee remained. The area was so sensitive I could hardly bear to have the covers touch it when I lay in bed. When I was standing up or walking, it was less painful. (I still had numbness in this area two and a half years later.)

I saw Dr. Spruce before returning to work. She scheduled me for an MRI of my back. She also referred me to a neurologist to check for permanent nerve damage to my leg and an orthopedic surgeon to evaluate the extent of my back injury and any treatments he deemed necessary. She sent me to a physical therapist for symptom relief and to learn appropriate exercises to strengthen my back muscles. These appointments wouldn't begin until after the New Year holiday.

I returned to work on December 20, wearing a back brace and being extremely careful of every movement I made.

THE DOWNHILL SLOPE

JANUARY AND FEBRUARY WERE BUSY months. I was having physical therapy treatments twice a week. I had the MRI and saw the neurologist and the orthopedic surgeon; each of these appointments required a trip to Las Cruces. The neurologist found I had no permanent nerve damage to my leg. The physical therapy was helpful, and by the time I saw the surgeon, I was feeling normal and without pain.

The MRI and X-rays showed I had some deterioration of the spine in my lower back, but the doctor said as long as I was having no current problems, there was no need to do anything. He wanted to see me immediately if I had a recurrence of pain or in a year for follow-up. I seemed to have recovered remarkably well from the whole back injury ordeal.

However, Robert was becoming more and more debilitated. His speech was grossly impaired—so slurred and faint that we were using a slate for communication. But his handwriting became so small, it was illegible. So I made an alphabet line so he could point to spell words. We had to play twenty questions to be able to decipher a thought. Mostly I would talk to him and frame his reply in a question so he could respond with a yes or a no.

He had stopped playing the piano. His fingers just didn't seem to work well anymore. Also I think his memory was failing; he could no longer remember the words, so he wasn't able to play the melody line.

His coordination had become so poor that he wasn't able to operate his new scooter when it arrived. He could no longer stand and transfer from bed to chair and back. He had fallen several times attempting to transfer by himself, so he had to call for assistance. His transfers had to be made using an electric lift and two nursing assistants.

It was no longer safe for him to use a standard wheelchair for transport. He needed a Geri chair, which is like a large recliner on wheels. He also had become incontinent of stool and urine. It took a long time for him to call for assistance to transfer and then get to the bathroom. Once he felt the urge to go, he rarely had enough control to hold it until he finally got to a bathroom.

I used to take him for scenic car rides on Sunday afternoons, but transfer problems meant we could no longer go for rides in the car. He had enjoyed being able to experience the outside world. We would usually stay within a twenty-mile radius of TorC; there were several lakes within that area we could easily visit. We would stop at McDonald's and go through the drive-thru to get a snack—usually an ice cream cone or a milk shake. Sometimes we would get a burger and fries also, and he would eat that in lieu of his supper at the Veterans Home. He had enjoyed these outings very much, but now he could no longer get in and out of my car. Instead, I would pick up food and bring it in as a treat.

As these multiple changes were occurring with Robert, my stress levels at work were increasing. Our census had grown—more than doubled—from when I had started, and I was being given more and more responsibility. It is required that certain duties be performed by a RN, and I was the only hospice RN. There were more admissions, more deaths, more medication changes, more equipment and care needs, and much more paperwork. I was working more hours per day and more days per week.

My increased workload and Robert's declining health were increasing my stress levels. So I took some steps to decrease my stress at work. I changed the days I worked; instead of working Monday, Tuesday, and Wednesday, I worked Sunday, Monday, and Tuesday, with Wednesday as a backup day if I needed it to finish paperwork, etc. Weekends at most health care facilities are generally quieter and more relaxed than weekdays; there's usually less staff working, and no ancillary services are available.

I also came to work later in the morning—at ten rather than eight. Sometimes I would work in the early evening hours before patient bedtimes. I began to schedule my assisted-living patients in the afternoon; often they participated in activities in the morning, and I would have to go back later to see them. I scheduled home visits much like a tour, using an efficient route to see my in-home patients without backtracking and crisscrossing the same areas. I planned the route so I could begin and end close to my house or close to the office. These changes helped a great deal.

In April, Robert suffered a bout of pneumonia. He had a high fever and was very fatigued; he stayed confined to his bed for about a week. He was put on oxygen and given antibiotics, and he rallied fairly well. However, it seemed to mark a turning point in his general health. He remained on the oxygen (via nasal cannula), and they changed his diet to pureed foods and thickened liquids. He was moved to the area in the dining room where patients could receive a great deal of assistance with eating; he was having trouble getting the food from his plate to his mouth. His tremors were becoming more severe and occurring more frequently.

The bout of pneumonia also seemed to create a change in Robert's attitude. He was much more subdued and wanted to spend more time in bed. He had little appetite and didn't seem to care much about eating. He lost a great deal of weight. Most of his interactions and communications were now through gestures and eye contact; he attempted very little verbal communication.

One aspect of my job was to determine eligibility for hospice. I decided to apply the criteria to Robert. I had been seeing changes in his behavior and his care needs, but I had never thought of him in terms of qualifying for hospice status. He fit the criteria in all areas!

It was like I had been suddenly thrust into a new reality. I had never thought of him as being a hospice candidate—of being terminal. Diabetes and Parkinson's disease are both chronic illnesses, and the complications from them do lead to conditions that are terminal, but Robert? Terminal? Oh my god!

The realization was quite a shock. But when I gave his situation further consideration, I realized that everything pointed to hospice. He was becoming increasingly debilitated and losing more and more of his abilities to function; he needed total care. I concluded I had a hospice patient in *my own family*. It was Robert, and his time was limited. I wanted to be able to spend more time with him while I still could.

I needed to resign from my job.

BARELY HANGING ON

IT WAS NEARLY THE END of April. I decided I would give Dottie a six-week lead to find my replacement. I handed her my resignation letter at our weekly staff meeting on Friday, May 2, to be effective June 10, the day before my seventy-second birthday. I would just have to hang on until June 10 and try to juggle work and my private life as best as I could.

I wanted Robert's time to include as much quality time as possible. The roses were in bloom in the garden—that first full flush of color in the spring, with dozens of flowers on each and every bush. The yard was beautiful. I made arrangements with the Activities Department to have Robert transported via wheelchair to the house in the facility van. Two staff members would assist him. I wanted him to see how beautiful the garden looked, how magnificent the fruits of his labor were to behold.

I had gone to McDonald's and had his favorite shake, burger, and fries meal for him to enjoy on the patio. The weather was beautiful that day, and he was supposed to arrive at about two o'clock in the afternoon. I waited and waited, but he didn't come. Finally, I called the Veterans Home to check on him. They told me that when staff went to put him in the van, he refused to go. So they canceled the trip.

I took his snacks and went to visit him. He was in his room. He said he had thought he was supposed to go at four o'clock, so he wouldn't go with them earlier. I was *so* disappointed he hadn't been able to see the yard. I thought it would give him a sense of pride to see its beauty.

We sat together in a dining area, and he ate his snacks. As we talked some more about the failed plans of the afternoon, I realized he didn't go to the house in the van because he was afraid to leave the facility; he felt safe and secure inside the Home with his big Geri chair, oxygen, and familiar space and staff. "Outside of the Home" was now a frightening place.

I told him I would take some pictures of the back yard and bring him copies so he could see how beautiful it was. I also said I would bring bouquets for him to give the staff and residents. I wouldn't try to schedule anything for him outside the Home again.

I told Robert that I was getting so overwhelmed with work that I had resigned; the day before my birthday would be my last workday. Then I would be able to spend more time with him. He said he liked that idea.

The days of May seemed to pass quickly. Memorial Day was celebrated on May 26 that year. I had to work Sunday, but we spent the holiday together. They had an outdoor cookout for the residents to attend. However, there was little that Robert could eat or wanted to eat in a pureed form. He wasn't feeling much like celebrating. He could no longer feed himself at all. His problem with swallowing was increasing. Even the thickened liquids would often make him cough or choke.

I worked Tuesday and Wednesday but visited him again on Thursday afternoon and stayed that evening until he was ready for bed. I told him I would be back the next afternoon to have supper with him and read him the comics.

I kissed him good-bye and said, "Nite, nite, termite. I'll see ya later, alligator."

"In a while, crocodile," he answered haltingly.

"I love you," I replied as I turned to leave.

"Ditto," he whispered.

The next day at about one, as I was driving home from our Friday-noon staff meeting, I got a call from Robert's nurse at the Home. He had experienced a "spell" during lunch in the dining room. He was now in bed on increased oxygen and resting quietly, but he appeared to be in a coma. I told them I would come there immediately.

TILL DEATH US DO PART

. . . .

I DROVE DIRECTLY TO THE facility and went straight to Robert's room. He was lying in bed, covered to the waist with a sheet, his chest naked. He had a nasal cannula with oxygen running at a very high rate. His eyes were closed, and he wasn't responsive to verbal stimuli. I looked at him, and I knew he was in his final stage of life; he was dying.

I reacted as a nurse; I had my hospice bag with me, so I took Robert's vital signs and did a full-body assessment. I knew the nurses on duty had already done this, but I felt so helpless. I wanted *to do something* for him. I wanted to know for sure what his physical status was.

He had a fever, but everything else appeared normal—except he was unresponsive. I talked to the nurse on duty. She said this spell was similar to others he'd had, but he usually didn't lose consciousness, and if so only momentarily.

She felt he might have aspirated some liquid into his lungs during lunch.

She made sure there were no changes I wanted to make to his living will. He was to receive comfort measures only: oxygen to facilitate breathing, pain and fever medications, and personal care. He wanted no feeding tubes, no IVs, no respirator or other life-prolonging equipment.

I told her I would stay with him for the rest of the day and call her if any changes occurred. They were giving him medication rectally to help bring down the fever. I put compresses on his head, neck, and underarms to help cool his body. He appeared to be resting comfortably.

I called Dottie to inform her of the situation. It was about three. I was scheduled to be on call for the weekend—starting at five on Friday until Monday at eight in the morning. She said she was very sorry to hear about Robert and told me not to worry about work; they would take care of it. I told her I would call and keep her informed of his status.

I pulled an easy chair along the side of the bed and held Robert's hand. I changed his compresses, wet his lips with ice chips, and swabbed his mouth with lemon swabs. I talked to him about what was on the TV. I played some music CDs for him. I stayed the rest of the day and through the night. Staff came in periodically to change him and turn him from side to side. They brought me a supper tray and later, during the night, some coffee.

Morning came, and activity on the unit increased; day shift staff entered to assess Robert and give him a bath and other care.

There had been no major change in his condition over the last eighteen hours. They didn't expect any changes in the next eight or more either. I decided to go home, sleep for a few hours, and come back in the afternoon.

I came back about three. Robert's condition was still unchanged. His fever would wax and wane. He was still on oxygen, and his breathing was regular and unlabored. He was changed and repositioned about every two hours. He didn't appear to be in any pain or discomfort, but he was totally unresponsive.

It has always been my belief that patients who are in a coma can still hear and are aware of things going on around them; they simply aren't able to respond to them in a visible way. Robert loved poetry, so I brought his favorite book of poems with me. He loved music, so I brought some of his favorite CDs for him to hear. We spent the evening and night together. I read him all of his favorite poems, played his favorite music, and "we" talked of memories and special places and people we'd known. I told him how much he had meant to me over the last quarter-plus century. I thanked him for all the love, acceptance, support, and comfort he had given me. I told him how much I would miss him, but I assured him I would be all right; he had helped me to learn the things I needed to know to carry on without him.

I told him I felt he would be just fine, too—no more pain or suffering or impairments. I reminded him of our many talks during which we speculated about life and death, and life after death. He had said he wasn't afraid of death; he felt his spirit or essence would live on. Only his physical body would cease its function; only his physical body would die. "He" (his spirit) would be freed to experience other realities in other worlds. He would exist in a state of love and peace. I said I felt that one day I would join him, and we would exist together in that place of love and peace.

I told him I had made the funeral arrangements we had agreed upon. He would be cremated, and I would scatter his ashes in several of our favorite places. I had written his obituary back in December 2005, when he had been in a coma. Any revisions needed would be minor.

I told him my daughters had offered to come and help me, but I had said I would prefer they save their leave time and take it later in the summer. I would make a visit to Florida once things were settled, and we could enjoy a happier time together.

I lay my head on his chest. I could hear his heart beating strongly and his even respirations—as though echoing in a cave. I knew these sounds would soon fade, and he would be gone from his body. I cried—sobbed—long and hard. I hugged his body and felt his warmth. I finally fell asleep on his chest. I awoke when staff came in to change and reposition him. They offered me some coffee, and I gratefully accepted. I felt drained and empty.

Sunday morning dawned, and after the change of shift, I went home to shower, eat, and rest. I returned about noon. There had been little change in Robert's condition for the last forty-eight hours, except that his bowels were no longer active, and his kidneys were putting out little or no urine. He appeared to be calm, comfortable, and resting peacefully.

The nurses encouraged me to go home and get a good night's sleep; they would get a sitter for Robert for the night, so he wouldn't be alone. There were some business items I needed to take care of Monday morning, so I agreed to that arrangement. I would stay until about nine, go home for the night, and return in the morning.

I spent the day at Robert's side, holding his hand, attending to his needs, talking with him, and playing some of his favorite music. At nine o'clock I kissed him good-night and said, "Rest well, my love. I'll see you in the morning."

I drove home and went right to bed. I was very tired, and it felt good to sleep in my own bed and at a normal bedtime hour. I slept very soundly.

I awoke to the ring of the telephone; it was six thirty. The nurse from the Home identified herself and said softly, "Mrs. Hildebrandt, Robert passed away at six twenty."

IN MEMORIAM
· ·

I FELT NUMB. I HAD known it was coming, but hearing that it had actually happened left me numb and empty. I called Charline, told her Robert had passed away early in the morning, and asked her to drive me to the Veterans Home at about eight. I didn't feel I was in any condition to drive a car, and I felt I needed some supportive TLC.

I called Dottie and told her of Robert's passing. I said I wouldn't be reporting for work again, but I would come in on Tuesday, June 10, to return keys and equipment. Dottie extended her condolences and asked if there was anything she could do to help. I thanked her and said I would call if I needed anything.

Charline came over, and we drove to the Home. I went straight to Robert's room. He was lying in the bed; he had been bathed and groomed and prepared by the staff for viewing. I gave Robert one last hug. He was still warm; I was glad of that. At least he didn't seem so *gone* that way. I kissed him, told him I loved him, and said one last good-bye.

I gathered his remaining personal items. Staff assisted me in getting his TV and radio-phonograph into Charline's car. Several of his caregivers came while I was there to say good-bye one last time and express condolences. I talked with the social worker, and we discussed a memorial service for Robert. We had talked previously about this but hadn't made any definite plans. We agreed to meet the next afternoon and finalize the arrangements. The service would be held on Friday, June 6.

After we left the Home, I delivered obituary notices to the two local papers. The papers came out on Tuesday afternoon, and the notice of his death would be in that week's edition. We went back to the house and unloaded the car. I asked Charline if she would call the kids and let them know what had happened. She called and told them, and then I talked with them and gave them the details. It was very hard for me to say the words "Robert died this morning at six twenty," but after that had been said, I could talk about the events of the last couple of days. We also notified my sister and brother. I decided that I would write to friends and other relatives and send them a copy of the obituary from the paper. I would work on that over the next few days or so.

The next day I went to see the social worker, and we planned Robert's memorial service. It would be at two in the main social room of the Veterans Home. I asked one of the residents who had been a rabbi in the military and was a friend of Robert to deliver the eulogy. Robert would have liked that.

One of the social workers would read the obituary. Robert's social worker would play the guitar and sing two of his favorite songs: "Morning Has Broken" and "The Rose." I had a tape of Robert playing his favorite songs on the piano. We would play it at the beginning and ending of the service. I would bring some flowers from the garden and also some bouquets the children were sending. I compiled a storyboard of Robert's life with pictures of him from various stages. The VA kitchen staff would provide cookies and beverages for those attending.

The sixth of June was hot like only a June day in New Mexico can be. As I was getting ready for the memorial service, I tugged and wiggled to get into my panty hose. I thought, *Robert would have laughed and said, "Don't bother."*

The meeting room was homey and had a comfortable feeling; it had dark-wood appointments with burgundy leather sofas and chairs, a fireplace wall with a mantle and bookshelves, a carpeted floor, and warm-colored drapes. It was a perfect place for a last tribute to Robert. There were friends and neighbors, work colleagues, and residents and staff from the Home; the guests overflowed into the hall outside. It was simple, but warm and personal. Robert would have liked it; I'm sure he did.

LIFE AFTER DEATH

. . . .

THERE MOST ASSUREDLY IS LIFE after death for those left behind. Life goes on. My days after Robert's death were filled initially with writing notes and letters to friends and relatives, notifying them of his passing, as well as thank-you notes to those who had been so kind and helpful to both of us during our difficult journey. I also started journaling, because I knew it would help me to grieve in a healthy way. These activities were very therapeutic for me.

I began to go through Robert's clothing. I left the clothes that were at the Home to be given to other residents. However, he had several boxes of winter clothing in the garage. Charline and I delivered these remaining items to the facility's tailor shop. They would find a new owner for all Robert's belongings, some of which were brand-new. This also was therapeutic for me.

There was paperwork to complete regarding Robert's death, agencies to be notified, death certificates to be enclosed, etc. However, this process was much simpler because of the paperwork I had done previously for Medicaid.

I had kept up the payments on Robert's life insurance policy, and I converted the death benefit monies to a guaranteed lifetime annuity. The monthly amount was small but was enough to elevate my monthly income to above survival level and allow me to watch my utilities less closely and feel like I could splurge on a new blouse or pair of shoes without having to cut something else out of my budget. I had saved most of my earnings from the last nine months, and although my bank balance was small, it was a cushion for unexpected expenses. I'd lived so tight since qualifying Robert for Medicaid that my new financial situation made me feel like I'd won the lottery. That's an exaggeration, but I did feel much more secure and felt I wouldn't need to find a job to survive each month. This was very comforting to me.

I scheduled a trip to Florida in July for two and a half weeks. I would see all my kids and grandkids and friends there. My sister and brother-in-law were in Michigan for the summer, so I wouldn't see them on this trip. As usual, I was treated royally and received copious amounts of love—and I luxuriated in its warmth.

While in Gainesville, Mary, a longtime friend, and I had lunch together. We were catching each other up on the latest events of our lives. She and her husband had recently experienced some traumatic health issues, and I shared some of the problems I had encountered with Robert and what I had done to cope with them. She suggested that I write a book relating my experiences of the last four years and what

I'd done to survive. She had been in public relations prior to retirement and had done some published writing earlier in her life. She still was skilled in the motivational, persuasive salesmanship that had made her successful in her career.

She pointed out that my background gave me credibility—I was an RN, a mental health clinical nurse specialist, a gerontologist, and an educator. I had wanted to write a book since my late teens while in college, but I felt I hadn't lived enough to have anything meaningful to say. Well, I had recently lived a lot, and I *did* have something meaningful to say. I hoped it would be beneficial to those who might have to make a similar journey.

I had recently written in my journal that I felt I was in a state of anomie—feeling aimlessness and uncertain regarding my future. I started to seriously consider her suggestion. I told my daughters about what Mary had said, and they too, encouraged me to write my story. Debbie, who works as a PR person for a large corporation, even volunteered to be my editor and my agent to get it published and promoted. Sean challenged me to send him the first five chapters by Christmas. At the time, August was less than a week away.

When I got home, I continued to think about the idea. I finally decided I would make it a project. I had nothing in my life that seemed to be a real purpose or a fulfilling goal. Why not give it a try? At the very least, it would be a therapeutic journal of the long and lonely journey I had just traveled. Regardless of the ultimate outcome of the endeavor, it would be a win-win for me.

Since you're reading my words, one of my wildest, seemingly most outlandish and improbable dreams has come true. Since dreaming is free, and wonderfully freeing, I don't intend to stop dreaming when this manuscript is published. I've got many more dreams that I want to come true.

EPILOGUE

· ·

ONE DREAM THAT I'VE HAD for more than thirty-five years—
ever since I first laid eyes on it—has been to live near the
ocean. When we lived in Florida, we visited the beaches
of the Atlantic and the Gulf of Mexico frequently. It often
provided a place of respite for me. Every visit I've made to
Florida since moving to New Mexico has included a trip to
the ocean.

When I visit my son in San Francisco, I always spend
as much time on the ocean piers as I can. I love the smell of
the ocean air, the feel of the coastal breeze on my face, and
the sound of the surf washing the shore. I love walking on
the sandy beach. I love the big expanse of sky and water,
and the gorgeous sunrises and sunsets. I *just plain love* the
ocean and its beaches.

All my family members know how I feel and are aware of
my dream of living near the ocean. Robert and I often talked

of how to make my dream a reality, but we always came to the same conclusion: we couldn't afford property on the beach. Moving to New Mexico—the hot and dry desert—had made my dream seem even less likely to become a reality.

After Robert died, I had plenty of time to dream again—to envision everything I had ever wanted. Why not? I had read several books about asking the universe for what you want. They say if you really want what you ask for, you'll get it. So I asked to be able to live by the ocean—a place with a big, wide beach and a view of mountains in the distance. There was much more to my dream, but the ocean was the setting.

I started telling my son, John, about my dream and what I was wishing my future would include. He told me, "It sounds to me like you're describing Santa Monica."

"I don't know," I said. "I've never been there. Where is it?"

"It's in California—on the coast—near LA. It's where Nikki's mother lived. You can see the mountains in the distance. It's a beautiful area."

"Well, if it's in California, I can't afford it."

"If you can afford to live where you are, you could afford to live in Santa Monica. Food and rent would be your two biggest expenses. You wouldn't be able to eat out all the time; you'd have to cook and eat in. So you could afford it if the rent was right." Then he said in an off-hand manner, "I could make the rent right. [John and his wife own an apartment building in Santa Monica just four blocks from the ocean.] Think about it. Sounds like the first step to making your dream come true. Let me know when you want to move there."

I was overwhelmed. I went to the atlas to see where Santa Monica was. Then I started to think about making such a move. What a change it would be! And how much work it would be. How foolish to think of doing such a thing at my age—seventy-four. Everyone I knew in TorC planned to live there for the rest of his or her life. They love the quiet, the lack of traffic, the weather, and the predictability.

I considered these elements. New Mexico weather is great—except during the two or three months of the windy season in the spring and the three months of summer when the temperature hovers around the one-hundred-degree mark every afternoon. Yes, it's quiet, and there's no traffic—because there's no place to go and nothing to do. Things do change there, but ever so slowly. If you aren't mindful, you might not notice the changes when they do occur. And lastly, there's security in predictability. But you could argue that the lack of change and excessive predictability made for a very stagnating environment.

I realized that the very elements that had attracted Robert and me to TorC were now things I found objectionable. Yet TorC hadn't really changed; my *attitude* about TorC had changed. My circumstances had changed, and now I wanted something different. I wanted to live where things were active and vital, where attitudes were young and fresh, and where change was happening. I wanted to live my dream to its fullest.

I went to Santa Monica for a visit for a week in November 2009. The place in my vision—my dream—looked just like Santa Monica. I walked the beach and enjoyed the ocean. I sat in the promenade, enjoyed coffee, and people watching. I sought out grocery stores and shopping areas within walking distance. I found a library, a YMCA, and a college offering interesting free classes to elderly residents—all within walking distance of the apartment house. I saw the apartment layout and visualized how my furniture might fit. I fell in love with the area, and I wanted to live there.

Although I'm predominately Gemini in my horoscope, I have a large dose of Taurus. This seems to provide a sort of check and balance for me. My Gemini is all for "follow you dream *now*," but my Taurus warns, "Don't burn your bridges before you're sure." So I went to Santa Monica in September 2010 for a four-month trial period. Six weeks later, I came back to TorC to put my house on the market, pack my belongings, and permanently move to Santa Monica. I would begin living my dream and fulfilling the many other aspects of that dream. I'd be setting out on another journey soon—literally riding off into the sunset.

Bon voyage!

ACKNOWLEDGMENTS

I WANT TO THANK MY many cheerleaders along the way—both friends and family—for their encouraging words of support. I send a big hug and thank-you to Sean for his initial wager, and to Debbie for proofreading and providing feedback in the early stages of writing. I want to especially thank my friend Gary, who came to my rescue when my computer skills were lacking and encouraged me when I doubted myself the most. Also, thanks to Sarah Beach Handy for her creative options for the cover design. Through their collective support, I'm on the path to realizing my dream and hopefully helping others along the way. That's the best scenario!

AUTHOR'S NOTE

. . . .

The Evolution of *Barely Hanging On*

IN THE MONTHS AFTER ROBERT'S death, my friends and family urged me to write a book sharing my caregiving experiences and my journey through a maze of social systems. They said it would help others who are struggling, those who could use the information and would find support in my story. Others would know they aren't alone.

I thought about their suggestions. I had always dreamed of writing a book, but honestly, I never felt my experiences qualified as book material. However, if they were right—if telling my story in book form would validate the experiences of other caregivers, support their struggle with conflicting emotions and frustrations, and be a resource for directing them on their path, it would be a worthwhile project to take on.

Best scenario: I write my story. The book is a success. It helps people on their journey. *And* my dream of being a book author is fulfilled. Worst scenario: The process of writing/journaling my story would be therapeutic for me. It would help me to grieve and then be able to move on in a positive and healthy way. So I decided to do it; I would share my story, and I would write it in book form. It was a win-win situation for me, regardless of the final outcome.

The latter outcome—positively moving on—has been realized. At seventy-five, I relocated and invented a new lifestyle. I'm living in Santa Monica, California, managing an apartment complex, taking college classes, and working as a part-time health care provider.

Putting my story in book form has taken a long time. I finished writing the manuscript in the first two years after Robert's death. However, it has lain dormant on my bookshelf as I became involved in transitioning into my new world in California. I'll soon be having my eightieth birthday; that means it has been nearly five years since I finished the original draft. I realized that it was probably *now or never*.

So I've recently started on another adventure into unknown territories: becoming the published author of a best-selling (hopefully) book. Since you're reading this, I'm on my way toward realizing my dream.